The Essential Guide
to Your Favourite Cocktail

CAES

CARS

Clint Pattemore

with food recipes by Connie DeSousa and John Jackson
and photography by Ryan Szulc

appetite
by RANDOM HOUSE

Appetite by Random House® is a registered trademark of Random House LLC

*MOTT'S, CLAMATO, MOTT'S CLAMATO THE WORKS, CLAMATO RIMMER and MR & MRS T
are trademarks used under licence by Canada Dry Mott's Inc.

Library and Archives of Canada Cataloguing in Publication is available upon request

ISBN: 978-0-449-01648-0
eBook ISBN: 978-0-449-01649-7

Image on page 11 © Gibson Smith Photography
Book design by CS Richardson

Printed and bound in Canada

Published in Canada by Appetite by Random House®,
a division of Random House of Canada Limited,
a Penguin Random House Company
www.randomhouse.ca

10 9 8 7 6 5 4 3 2 1

To Caesar fans everywhere. Cheers!

Contents

Hello Caesar fans!

. . . .

Welcome to my world of Caesars! In this book, I'm very excited to share my thoughts, ideas, and recipes for Canada's cocktail. Since my first experience making and tasting the Caesar's savoury tomato-clam mixture, as a rookie bartender on a riverboat, I have had a real fondness for this most Canadian of cocktails.

Now, as the Caesar Mixing Officer (CMO) for Mott's* Clamato*, I get to spread what I call the "Caesar love" across Canada and meet die-hard Caesar fans all over this great country. I am continually blown away by how passionate Canadians are about this cocktail—and now I get to share this passion with you!

The cocktail recipes in this book have been created simply, using common grocery store ingredients and basic drink-making techniques. They are designed to show you new ways to make your favourite Caesar, and to inspire you to get creative (and a little unconventional!) at home. Of course, there will always be purists who will drink only the classic version, and that's all right with me—hey, it's the classic for a reason, right? But I hope I can show you how the classic recipe also acts as a great platform to highlight other ingredients and flavours.

There are lots of hints and tips on how to make variations of each cocktail recipe throughout the book, so use them as guidelines and build upon them. My hope is that you will try the Caesars I've created, then take those ideas and make them your own. Once you find the ingredients and ratios that taste best to you, share them with others, and help me to keep converting non-Caesar drinkers into new fans.

Happy mixing—let's spread the Caesar love!

Clinton Pattemore
@CaesarClint

Hail Caesar!
The Story of Canada's Cocktail

The year 1969 was an exciting one in Canada. Bell-bottoms were all the rage. Winnipeg rockers The Guess Who topped the charts with "These Eyes," and John Lennon played his first post-Beatles concert with the Plastic Ono Band in Toronto. The Montreal Expos played their first home game, bringing Major League Baseball to Canada. And, in Calgary, a bartender mixed up a tasty new concoction that would go on to become Canada's cocktail: the Caesar.

That man was Walter Chell. He worked as a restaurant manager at the Owl's Nest bar in what was then the Calgary Inn and is now the Westin Calgary. He was asked to come up with a new cocktail to celebrate the opening of the hotel's new eatery, Marco's Italian Restaurant, and chose to name it Caesar, after the great Roman emperor. Working off the new restaurant's menu, Chell based his new aperitif on the rich and complex flavours of one of the dishes, Spaghetti Vongole (spaghetti with clams). His cocktail creation featured a flavour profile of sweet (tomato juice), salty (clam nectar), sour (lime), savoury (Worcestershire sauce), and bitter (celery salt). The Duffy-Mott Company made life easier for bartenders and Caesar lovers alike by introducing Mott's Clamato Cocktail, a cocktail mixer combining all these flavours, later that same year.

The Caesar has since evolved from its strictly vodka-based beginnings to include a myriad of spirit, spice, and flavour combinations—all anchored by the indispensable ingredient of Mott's Clamato Cocktail—and its popularity has kept on growing. In a 2006 survey conducted by the CBC, the Caesar was voted the 13th greatest Canadian invention of all time, and in 2009, while celebrating the 40th anniversary of the Caesar, the Canadian Parliament declared it Canada's National Cocktail. More than 350 million Caesars are now enjoyed by Canadians each year! We just can't get enough of this true taste of Canada.

Entertaining with Caesars

· ·

All cocktails have a built-in sociability to them. They're designed to be admired, enjoyed, savoured, and celebrated in the company of friends and family. They are the classic accessory—or, *s'il vous plaît, l'accoutrement*—to good times. And yet, the Caesar is somehow in a class of its own. The vibrant colours and flavours of the classic recipe or any of its ever-evolving variations, accented with a bold and unique rim and an endless array of possible garnishes—all combine to produce a cocktail that is as much a piece of art as it is an achievement in mixology. And that is what this book is all about: capturing that mysterious yet so familiar essence that is Canada's cocktail—the perfect additional element to good friends, good food, and good times.

The savoury, bold character of the Caesar cries out for tasty food dishes to accompany it, so along with the cocktail recipes in this book, there are also food recipes to enjoy with them. These recipes were created by Connie DeSousa and John Jackson, the co-owners and co-executive chefs of Calgary's CHARCUT Roast House. Connie and John believe in value, sustainability, creativity, and the promise food holds for community, both local and global, and they've enjoyed a rush of critical and guest accolades for their urban-rustic fare. The food at Charcut Roast House is "back-to-basics" fare, expertly prepared, fresh and from scratch. Oh, and a sign that they're perfect to write the food recipes for this book: one of the places they worked together early in their careers was the Owl's Nest—the very establishment where Walter Chell first created the Caesar!

Anatomy of a Caesar

. . . .

In this section we break down the Caesar into its individual elements and examine exactly what goes into making Canada's cocktail. We take a look at traditional ingredients, from rimmers (also known as rimming salt) to garnishes, and explore opportunities to get creative with the classic Caesar.

Rimmers

Unlike that other tomato cocktail (you know which one I'm talking about!), Caesars are well known for the distinctive brown celery salt dusting around the rim of each glass. Celery salt prepares our taste buds for the savouriness of the tomato-clam mixture that follows: the celery seed and salt combination gives your lips and tongue a quick pungent, bitter flavour hit before they reach the savoury sweetness of the drink itself. The other beautiful thing about celery salt is that it works well with so many flavours: you can combine it with almost any dried herbs and spices—from oregano to allspice to wasabi—to create an endless variety of rimmers.

To keep things simple, most of the rimmer recipes in this book use one of the following:

- **Celery salt:** the original rimmer. This is great on its own but also works well with other herbs and spices. Don't forget to check out the Mott's Clamato Rimmer*—a unique blend of celery salt with added herbs and spices.

- **Fresh cracked salt and black pepper:** basic seasoning mixture of coarse sea salt and black peppercorns ground together. The rimmer recipes in this book use a 1:1 ratio of salt to pepper. This is also a great base to add other flavours into the mix.

- **Montreal steak spice:** another Canadian favourite with a one-of-a-kind taste. It adds a coarse texture and volume to the rimmer as well.

When a combination of spices are used in the rimmer, the ratio of the measurements are given in the recipe. You'll find directions for rimming a glass on page 18.

Ice

The most underrated ingredient in cocktails is ice, yet it is one of the most important. Generally, you want to use the same amount of ice as there is liquid, which is why you should always use a full glass of ice. More ice in the glass means it will get colder faster, and will stay colder longer. Drinks with only a little ice in them don't get cold enough to start with, so the ice melts much more quickly and dilutes the drink. Some people prefer minimal or no ice, but if you like a strong drink that stays cold and doesn't dilute your creation, use a full glass of ice.

Whole cubes—1-inch (2.5 cm) cubes from regular ice trays—are used in most of the drink recipes, though they're smashed up and put into a blender for the frozen Caesar cocktails (pages 74–77).

Alcohol

Choosing the alcohol to use in your Caesar is of great importance. Although vodka is used in the original recipe and is the most commonly used alcohol for Caesars, it doesn't have to be the only option. Vodka has little or no flavour to it (unless it's been flavoured), so by switching to a different spirit (gin, rum, whisky, or tequila, for example), you immediately add another layer of flavour to the Caesar. You'll find a detailed list of the main alcohols featured in the cocktail recipes in the Alcohol in Caesars chapter, pages 191–4, as well as tips on infusing alcohol with different flavours.

Non-Alcoholic Options

Although the Caesar is typically made with alcohol, it also makes for a great virgin cocktail, since it's already packed with flavour. The cocktail recipes in the book can be easily made non-alcoholic by simply leaving out the spirit. Non-alcoholic versions are great for all ages to enjoy.

Seasoning

The second essential ingredient in a Caesar is some sort of seasoning, whether it's simple salt and pepper, a light flavourful heat, or the most outrageously hot of hot sauces. I am always on the lookout for ways to add to or complement the flavour of that particular drink without overwhelming the rest of the cocktail. A great Caesar has a perfect balance of spice and flavour.

Salt and Pepper

Just as you would season your food, salt and pepper help balance and enhance the flavour of your Caesar. Fresh ground sea salt and cracked black pepper will yield the most flavour but, in a pinch, table salt and pepper will work. There are a lot of variations of sea salts and flavoured salts as well as different types of peppercorns available. Be sure to check out the international section of your grocery store for ideas and inspiration.

Hot Sauces

These days, choices for hot sauces are limitless. Thanks to the Internet, we have access to hot sauces made with every kind of pepper or chili imaginable, and hot sauces infused with various ingredients, including fruits, vegetables, and spirits. Most of the Caesar recipes in this book call for jalapeño hot sauce (a tasty green sauce with a delicate heat and lots of flavour) or a cayenne or Tabasco pepper–based hot sauce (sauces with strong heat, and used more for adding heat than flavour). These are the most common hot sauces used with Caesars in Canada, and on the Scoville heat scale, they are among the less spicy varieties. Occasionally I'll suggest chipotle hot sauce, when I'm looking to add a level of smoky flavour—and sometimes, the hottest you have (HYH) hot sauce, when it's time to go crazy! Feel free to experiment with your favourite blends.

Worcestershire Sauce

Worcestershire sauce, often known as "worch," is one of my favourite ingredients in a Caesar. It is a classic sauce for preparing meats and some savoury dishes, as well as a staple in every bar in Canada (thanks to the popularity of the Caesar). The best Worcestershires have spent time fermenting, which allows them to take on several flavours, and produce what can be a very complex taste. Don't be shy with the worch in your Caesars—a healthy four to five dashes adds a salty and savoury element that is hard to duplicate with other ingredients.

Other Sauces

Worcestershire sauce is typically used with meats as a marinade and works excellently in a Caesar, so it makes perfect sense that other steak or BBQ sauces would also complement the flavours of Canada's cocktail. Most are a bit thicker in consistency and sometimes need to be thinned out, with water, juice, or even alcohol, for easier mixing. The next time you're in your local grocery store, check out the multitude of other sauces available to you—soy sauce, fish or oyster sauce, tamarind, or even more exotic sauces like ponzu are all excellent choices for Caesars! Each sauce offers its own flavour profile to play with and make your Caesar unique.

Mott's Clamato Cocktail

This is definitely the most important ingredient when it comes to making a Caesar, and a staple in most Canadian pantries. Mott's Clamato Cocktail comes in four varieties:

- **Mott's Clamato Original:** This is the tomato-clam cocktail that you know and love. Seasoned with just the right balance of spices, Mott's Clamato Original is what gives the Caesar cocktail its unmistakable savoury taste.

- **Mott's Clamato Extra Spicy:** The name says it all. This variety is for those who enjoy their Caesar on the decidedly hot side. Mott's Clamato Extra Spicy delivers the same one-of-a-kind flavour of Mott's Clamato Original but has an added measure of spices and peppers to add sizzle to any recipe.

- **Mott's Clamato The Works*:** The Works takes the Mott's Clamato Original base and adds a balanced blend of seasonings, extra spices, and peppers, along with the flavour and heat of horseradish, to deliver a robust and zesty cocktail like no other.

• **Mott's Clamato Ready-to-Drink Caesar:** For those times when you just want to open up a bottle and enjoy, a Mott's Clamato Ready-to-Drink Caesar comes expertly mixed and ready to go with the vodka already added! It is also a great mixer for any vodka-based Caesar recipe. Choose from the classic Original or Extra Spicy.

Any of these four varieties will work in the recipes in this book, with each bringing its own characteristics to the cocktail. There's no right or wrong way when mixing with Mott's Clamato Cocktail—only *your* way!

Garnishes

When it comes to cocktails, a person drinks with their eyes first— and no other part of the Caesar plays to the first two senses (sight and smell) quite like the garnish. From something as simple as a stalk of celery to over-the-top oysters on the half shell, the garnish is where it's at! The truth is, you can garnish a Caesar with pretty much anything you want: if you like it and it tastes good, just do it!

The more you can tie the flavour of the garnish back to the flavour of the ingredients in the drink, the better. There are many recipes in the book that use the flavours of the garnish in the drink itself. For example, in the Caesar Fresa, strawberries and cilantro are muddled, while a berry and sprig are also used as the garnish. The same goes for the Maple BBQ Caesar, where BBQ sauce goes into the drink and is also brushed onto the maple bacon knots, then skewered for the garnish.

What follows is a list of the most common garnishes called for in the book. You'll find more information on how to prepare these for the recipes starting on page 21.

Citrus

Citrus is used in cocktails all over the planet. It was originally mixed with spirits as a remedy for common sicknesses back in the days of scurvy, but nowadays it's added to balance the sweetness of drinks, and so many people love the citrusy sour flavour. Limes, lemons, and oranges are the most popular, but other types, such as grapefruit and tangerines, also work well. Citrus wedges, wheels, and twists are the garnishes most often used in the recipes (see pages 21–23).

Other Fruits and Vegetables

Most fruits and veggies—from apples and peaches to cucumbers and zucchini—make great garnishes, as they are appealing to the eye, edible, and usually complement the flavours in the Caesar. Feel free to skewer your favourite fruit and vegetable, whether raw, grilled, cooked, or even pickled (store-bought or homemade), and place them atop the drink.

Herbs and Spices

Tucking sprigs of fresh herbs like dill, rosemary, or cilantro into the top of your Caesar adds an aesthetic touch but also brings interesting and delicate aromas that can enhance flavours in the drink that you may not have tasted otherwise. Sprinkling fresh or dried spices over top the drink, or adding them to the rimmer, can have the same effect. A couple of cracks of fresh black pepper over the Caesar is a personal favourite of mine.

Seafood

Probably the most natural garnish for Caesars is seafood, since the cocktail already contains an element of shellfish flavour. We're lucky in Canada to have access to some of the best seafood in the world. Clams, mussels, lobster, shrimp, and oysters all go well with a Caesar, so the next time you're serving them as appetizers or for dinner, double them up as your Caesar garnish.

Meat

Any Caesar fan who isn't also a fan of the meat garnish must be crazy! Meat is a match made in heaven for our favourite savoury cocktail. If you are cooking a nice steak, roasting a chicken, frying some bacon, or preparing any other meat that would pair well with a Caesar, don't be afraid to serve it up alongside.

Caesar-Making Equipment and Techniques

· ·

In this chapter, I explain all the techniques used to make a variety of Caesars and discuss the key equipment you'll need, so that you're all set to prepare Caesars at home, for yourself and your guests.

Glassware

The most important part of any cocktail is the vessel from which to drink. Most Canadians I know have their own special Caesar glass, whether it's a highball or pint glass, a Mason jar, or 32-oz (946 mL) schooner mug, and some use it religiously. I've seen some of the funkiest drinking vessels you can imagine (hollowed-out peppers and cucumbers come to mind), but strange as they have been, they all did the trick of getting the drink to my lips—and that's what counts!

Recipe Volume

Generally speaking, each Caesar recipe is designed to yield a single cocktail, except for those that allow guests to get hands-on and serve themselves, such as the Thanksgiving or 'Tis the Season Caesars. The volume that each Caesar recipe will produce is indicated with an icon. If you want to double-check the volume that your glass can hold, measure it using some water and a measuring glass before you begin. If you use a different-sized glass than the icon calls for, adjust the ingredient quantities accordingly.

Rocks	Highball	Pint	Flute	Margarita	Hurricane	Punch Bowl
9 oz	12 oz	16 oz	9 oz	8 oz	12 oz	150 oz
(265 mL)	(355 mL)	(475 mL)	(265 mL)	(235 mL)	(335 mL)	(about 4 L)

Measuring

I suggest that you use a proper shot glass or jigger to measure out the liquids in the cocktail recipes. A standard shot glass holds approximately 1 oz (30 mL). A jigger usually has two sides—one holding 1 oz (30 mL) and the other, 1½ oz (45 mL) or sometimes 2 oz (60 mL). The other tool I use for measuring liquid is a professional barspoon, which holds about ⅛ oz (3 mL). This measure is smaller than that of a typical teaspoon (5 mL), so keep this in mind when making the recipes.

I sometimes use the terms "dash" and "pinch" for measurements. For our purposes, a dash is the same as a barspoon—⅛ oz (3 mL). When it comes to dashing liquids from a bottle (those with a lid designed for dashing), I like to use a good healthy shake. The less liquid left in the bottle, the more that is likely to come out when you dash, so keep your eye on that. A "pinch" is what I use for dried herbs and spices, and is the amount you can grab with your thumb and forefinger. This is sometimes measured around 1/16 teaspoon (0.25 mL).

Rimming a Glass

One of the classic elements of the Caesar is the rimmed glass. Rimming a glass is a relatively simple process of moistening the edge of the glass, then rotating it through the rimmer you want it to adhere to. Citrus is one of the best and most commonly used liquids to moisten your rim—whether it's lime, lemon, orange, or any other type—due to the fact it contains naturally occurring sugar. The sugar acts as a bonding agent and ensures the rimmer will stick to the glass. Beware: plain water will make your rimmer soggy!

Rimmer is the first flavour to cross your lips. To rim a glass, moisten the rim by rubbing the fleshy side of a citrus wedge around it or simply dip it in any citrus juice. Next, dip the rim of the glass into a bowl or plate of rimmer mixture (see pages 7–8). Give the glass a quick shake or tap to remove any excess mixture. Rimming the entire mouth of the glass is not always necessary. Sometimes just a three-quarter rim or even a half-rim is made, mainly for people who don't like the rimmer but want their Caesars to have that classic look, or for those who want the option of drinking from either a rimmed or unrimmed glass.

Mixing a Caesar

A mixing glass is what you'll find me using to make most of my Caesars. Whether they're stirred, rolled, or muddled, I always prefer preparing them in one glass and serving them in another, with fresh cold ice or straight up. Any 16-oz (475 mL) glass with solid, thick glass will do for mixing.

Stirring

Probably the easiest and most common way to mix a Caesar is by stirring. Stirring will mix the drink and melt some of the ice, without agitating the liquids inside the glass too much. One of the keys to mixing up a good Caesar is the order in which you add the ingredients: I always go with ice first, then usually add the spirit(s) next, then the sauces and spices, and finally the rest of liquids, so that they can help carry the flavours down through the ice. There are no hard and fast rules though—you can do it in reverse, and if it still tastes good, that's all that matters! The easiest and best way to stir a cocktail is to move the spoon around the inside of the glass, spinning the ice in a circle. A good stir takes 30 to 45 seconds. A barspoon is very efficient for stirring—plus using it looks professional in front of your guests.

Rolling

Rolling is the midpoint between stirring and shaking a cocktail, and it's my favourite way to mix a Caesar. Rolling mixes the drink thoroughly, chilling and diluting it without infusing air or adding froth. You have probably rolled liquids before without knowing it: it's simply the action of pouring liquid from one glass to

another, back and forth a few times (three is my magic number). To prevent spillage, look at where you want the liquid to go, not at where it's coming from, and once you've started pouring *commit to the pour* to avoid dribbling liquid everywhere!

Shaking

A properly shaken cocktail will result in a little froth or some bubbles on the top of the drink, caused by the air that was forced into the liquid by this action. I always give my bottle of Mott's Clamato a good shake before opening it. I do not recommend shaking the Caesar itself, though, as it can alter the appearance and texture of the drink.

Muddling

When it comes to adding new ingredients to drinks and infusing flavours, nothing works better than muddling. You can muddle *anything*: citrus fruits (limes, lemons, oranges) and fresh soft fruits (grapes, pineapple, berries), herbs (basil, sage, cilantro), and spices (cloves, allspice, seeds). All it involves is a mixing glass, your chosen ingredients, and a muddler. If you don't have a muddler, a wooden spoon, rolling pin, or any clean cylindrical object will work. Just as if making a Mojito, you want to press and squeeze the ingredients so that they will release their flavours into the glass. This takes a little elbow grease, but the end product is sure to be delicious. When it comes to presentation, you can choose to leave the muddled ingredients in the drink or strain them out, for a cleaner-looking Caesar. To each their own!

Straining

Not every drink needs to be strained, but if you like your drinks straight up (no ice), then you'll need a strainer. Also, if you're like me and want your drink served as cold as possible, with little dilution, mixing it in one glass and then straining it into another glass filled with fresh ice will make a world of difference.

Blended Caesars

Most people enjoy their Caesars really cold, so why not make them frozen? We are in Canada, after all! All you need is a good blender and plenty of crushed ice to go with your chosen ingredients. Just wrap some ice cubes in a tea towel and bang them with a rolling pin. You can make the frozen Caesar slushies (pages 74–77) even more savoury by adding chopped-up herbs or spices. To get the desired consistency or smoothness, add the liquid to a blender about half full of crushed or broken up ice, and add more ice as needed. Remember, you can always add more ice, but you can't take it away.

Caesar Floats

A float is a drizzling of liquid—such as red wine or whisky—over top the mixed Caesar. This can be done for appearance, taste, or texture. To add a float to a Caesar, simply place your thumb or forefinger loosely over the mouth of the spout or bottle as you pour. This controls the amount of liquid that comes out—about ½ ounce (15 mL) is usually sufficient.

Garnishing a Caesar

The basic garnishes for Caesars are simple and easy to prepare; the techniques for creating them are described below. Remember to wash fruits and vegetables thoroughly, if using, and remove any stickers before preparing the garnish.

Skewering Garnishes

Skewers come in many styles. Wooden toothpicks, bamboo skewers (some with decoratively knotted ends), and metal cocktail picks are all popular tools to spear through a garnish. Your choice of skewer may depend on the size of the garnish. Smaller ones—less than 5 inches (12 cm)—should be laid atop the cocktail, whereas longer ones may be placed standing inside the drink.

Citrus Wedges

Citrus wedges are by far the most popular garnish when it comes to cocktails. With Caesars, a wedge is most commonly used to moisten the glass before putting on the rimmer, but it can also make a good garnish, for two reasons: it can be squeezed into the drink for added flavour, and it is very handy to use to swipe around the mouth of the glass to remove the rimmer when you've had enough!

How to cut citrus wedges:
1. Using a cutting board and paring knife, slice off the nub ends of the fruit, just to the pulp.
2. Set the fruit upright on the cutting board and slice it completely in half lengthwise. You'll see two lines of white membrane running down the centre of each half.
3. Gently score the middle of the lime across the membrane. This cut will allow the wedge to sit on the rim of the glass.
4. Cut each half of the fruit lengthwise again to get 4 equal-sized pieces, then cut each piece lengthwise in half again, for 8 equal-sized wedges. (If the fruit is small, you may need to cut each half into thirds instead of quarters, for a total of 6 wedges.)

Citrus Wheels

Like wedges, wheels perch on the rim of the glass, but they tend to sit up higher and make a big visual impact.

How to cut citrus wheels:
1. Using a cutting board and paring knife, slice off the nub ends of the fruit, just to the pulp.
2. Cut the fruit crosswise into ¼-inch (5 mm) thick slices.
3. Make a small cut in the middle of each slice, beginning near the centre, cutting outward through the rind.
4. If desired, cut the slice in half again to form a half-moon shape.

Citrus Twists

Twists can add flavour and aroma to your Caesar if you squeeze the oils from the rind over the top of the drink. Here are four easy ways to make various sizes and shapes of twists:

Peeled Twists
1. Using a potato or vegetable peeler, peel the skin of the citrus lengthwise to create strips.
2. Take the skin strip and twist into a spiral above the Caesar, spraying the citrus oils over the drink, then place it on top as a garnish.

Channel Twists
1. Using a channel knife, peel the fruit above the Caesar so that the oils that spray out land on the drink.
2. Take the peeled strip of citrus skin and twist it into a spiral above the Caesar, then place it on top as a garnish.

Wheel Twists
1. Take a citrus wheel and fillet the pith and rind from the skin, releasing the flesh.
2. Take the filleted citrus skin and twist it into a spiral above the Caesar, spraying the citrus oils onto the drink, then place it on top as a garnish.

Disc Twists
1. Using a paring knife, slice off the nub ends of the fruit.
2. Place the fruit so that it sits flat on the work surface and slice off loonie-sized discs of the peel.
3. Squeeze the oils from the disc of citrus skin onto the Caesar, then place the disc on top as a garnish.

Flamed Citrus Twists
You can flame citrus twists for a caramelized flavour and, of course, to show off a bit to your friends. Follow the method described above to create disc twists. With a disc held between your thumb and forefinger of one hand, hold a flaming match or lighter close to it but not touching, for 2 to 3 seconds, to warm up the peel. Then squeeze the peel, spraying the oils through the flame and onto the drink. The quicker the squeeze, the bigger the flame.

WARNING: Using fire is always dangerous, so do this carefully.

CAESAR

RECIPES

The Classic Caesar

························

This recipe is where it all began. Thank you, Walter Chell!

Glass

Rim Celery salt or Mott's Clamato Rimmer

What 1 oz (30 mL) vodka
2 dashes hot sauce
4 dashes Worcestershire sauce
3 grinds fresh cracked salt and pepper
4 oz (120 mL) Mott's Clamato Cocktail

Garnish Celery stalk
Lime wedge

How 1. Rim a highball glass with citrus and rimmer.
2. Fill the glass to the top with ice.
3. Add the ingredients in the order listed.
4. Stir well to mix the cocktail, and garnish.

SPR

Spring is the season of promise—the return of warmth, greenery, and the scents of the earth. This chapter focuses on clean, crisp flavours and recipes that feature the new season's crop

ING

of fresh ingredients. The Radish & Dill Caesar, the Blackberry Lemon Caesar—or any of the others, for that matter—will awaken your senses to vibrant, fresh taste combinations.

Caesar Sangrita

· ·

Not to be confused with the mixture of red wine, fruit juices, and brandy that is sangria, sangrita is the classic Mexican blend of orange juice and tomato juice, traditionally enjoyed while sipping a fine tequila. I took that flavour profile as the inspiration for this recipe, and used it to give Canada's cocktail a Mexican twist. Adding orange juice to a Caesar gives the cocktail a brightness and a sweet-sour citrus hit that makes it unlike anything you've tried before—not to mention that it pairs beautifully with the tequila.

Glass

Rim Fresh cracked salt and black pepper

What 2 dashes jalapeño hot sauce
2 grinds fresh cracked salt and black pepper
1½ oz (45 mL) fresh orange juice
1 oz (30 mL) 100% blue agave tequila
3 oz (90 mL) Mott's Clamato Cocktail

Garnish Orange wheel
Orange twist

How 1. Rim a highball glass with citrus and rimmer.
2. Fill the glass to the top with ice.
3. Add the ingredients in the order listed.
4. Stir well to mix the cocktail, and garnish.

· ·

Be sure to squeeze the twist over top the drink so that the oils enhance its aroma. Change up this Caesar by muddling fresh herbs like cilantro or rosemary in with some orange wedges instead of using the juice. Plus, orange isn't the only member of the citrus family that can be used here—try a tangerine or even grapefruit.

Scottish Spring Caesar

. . . .

With this Caesar I hoped to capture the essence of spring's first warm days on the Scottish island of Islay. I built it upon a big, smoky Scotch, coupled with pickled elements to represent the last of the winter's jarred goodies from the previous summer.

Glass

Rim   Fresh cracked salt and black pepper

What   6 dashes Worcestershire sauce
             3 dashes cayenne hot sauce
             3 grinds fresh cracked salt and black pepper
             ½ oz (15 mL) pickle brine (from any jar of pickled vegetables)
             1 oz (30 mL) Scotch
             3 oz (90 mL) Mott's Clamato Cocktail

Garnish Celery stick
             Pickled green tomato slice

How   1. Rim a highball glass with citrus and rimmer.
             2. Fill the glass to the top with ice.
             3. Add the ingredients in the order listed.
             4. Stir well to mix the cocktail, and garnish.

. . . .

This recipe is really tasty if you use a Scotch from the Isle of Islay with a strong peat-smoke flavour. Try switching the pickle brine for olive brine to bring a different flavour and give the Caesar that classic Dirty Martini taste and feel.

Royal Caesar

. . . .

This recipe was created in 2011 in honour of the royal wedding of William and Kate. Served in a flute, it's an elegant Caesar that radiates all things British. Built on the twin spirits of gin and the uniquely English Pimm's, it has a cool freshness woven in from the cucumber and a dash of bitters that creates a refreshing, easy-drinking, and classy cocktail.

Glass

Rim   Fresh cracked salt

What   1 slice cucumber
2 dashes Angostura bitters
3 grinds fresh cracked salt and black pepper
1 oz (30 mL) gin
1 oz (30 mL) Pimm's No. 1
4 oz (120 mL) Mott's Clamato Cocktail

Garnish   Cucumber slice
Fresh cracked salt and black pepper

How   1. In a mixing glass, muddle everything but the gin, Pimm's No. 1, and Mott's Clamato Cocktail.
2. Add the gin, Pimm's No. 1, and Mott's Clamato Cocktail, and stir well to mix and spread the flavours around.
3. Rim a flute and fill to the top with ice.
4. Strain the mixture into the flute, and garnish.

. . . .

To make this Caesar even closer to the classically British Pimm's Cup Cocktail, muddle lemon wedges and strawberries in with the cucumber. For a fancier, bubbly version, float your favourite champagne or sparkling wine on top.

Blackberry Lemon Caesar

. . . .

They might seem like strange bedfellows, but tomatoes and blackberries go really, really well together—the sweetness and acidity of the tomatoes complement the sweetness and fruitiness of the berries. Add plenty of cracked pepper to the mix and you get a refreshing balance of sweet and savoury.

Glass

Rim   Celery salt or Mott's Clamato Rimmer

What   5 blackberries
            2 lemon wedges
            2 dashes jalapeño hot sauce
            2 dashes Worcestershire sauce
            5 grinds fresh cracked black pepper
            1 oz (30 mL) gin
            4 oz (120 mL) Mott's Clamato Cocktail

Garnish Blackberries on a skewer

How   1. In a mixing glass, muddle everything but the gin and Mott's Clamato Cocktail.
            2. Add the gin and Mott's Clamato Cocktail, and stir well to mix and spread the flavours around.
            3. Rim a highball glass and fill to the top with ice.
            4. Strain the mixture into the highball glass, and garnish.

. . . .

The flavours of mint, ginger, cinnamon, and cloves also work well with tomatoes—these ingredients can be muddled in along with the blackberries, if you like. Or change up the lemon wedges for orange or peach slices, for a unique flavour.

Clamdigger Caesar

. . . .

Here's a simple Caesar for those who really enjoy the clam part of their Mott's Clamato Cocktail—I've bumped it up even more for this one with some extra clam nectar.

Glass

Rim   Celery salt or Mott's Clamato Rimmer

What
- 1 oz (30 mL) gin
- 2 dashes of your favourite hot sauce
- 2 dashes Worcestershire sauce
- 5 grinds fresh cracked black pepper
- 1 oz (30 mL) clam nectar
- 3 oz (90 mL) Mott's Clamato Cocktail

Garnish   Clams steamed in white wine, herbs, and Mott's Clamato Cocktail

How
1. Rim a highball glass with citrus and rimmer.
2. Fill the glass to the top with ice.
3. Add the ingredients in the order listed.
4. Stir well to mix the cocktail, and garnish.

. . . .

Feel free to use more clam nectar, for a bigger, clammier punch.

Mary Had a Little Lamb Caesar

One of the classic springtime family feast meats is fresh lamb. If you roast your lamb, use some of the jus left over from the roasting pan directly in the cocktail for delicious lamb flavour. If you prefer to grill your lamb, skewer some for a garnish. The red wine float adds a touch of dryness to the super savouriness of the Caesar.

Glass

Rim   Fresh cracked salt and black pepper

What   1 oz (30 mL) whisky
            4 dashes Worcestershire sauce
            2 dashes cayenne hot sauce
            5 grinds fresh cracked black pepper
            1 oz (30 mL) lamb jus
            4 oz (120 mL) Mott's Clamato Cocktail
            Float red wine

Garnish Grilled lamb on a skewer
            Sprig fresh mint

How   1. Rim a highball glass with citrus and rimmer.
            2. Fill the glass to the top with ice.
            3. Add the ingredients in the order listed.
            4. Stir well to mix the cocktail, and garnish.

Mint is a classic flavour pairing with lamb. Stick a sprig in the Caesar for garnish and added aroma, or muddle some into the glass before adding the ingredients for added fresh mintiness.

Radish & Dill Caesar

. . . .

Radishes go great with tomatoes and give this Caesar a nice spiciness, which is pulled right through the cocktail with the radish- and dill-infused gin. It's got some heat, but it's very refreshing, making it a terrific springtime sipper.

Glass

Rim　　Celery salt or Mott's Clamato Rimmer

What　　1 oz (30 mL) radish- and dill-infused gin (see below)
3 dashes jalapeño hot sauce
3 dashes Worcestershire sauce
3 grinds fresh cracked salt and black pepper
4 oz (120 mL) Mott's Clamato Cocktail

Garnish　Radish rose
Sprig fresh dill

How　　1. Rim a highball glass with citrus and rimmer.
2. Fill the glass to the top with ice.
3. Add the ingredients in the order listed.
4. Stir well to mix the cocktail, and garnish.

. . . .

Radish- and dill-infused gin is easily made by sealing 5 to 6 thinly sliced radishes and 2 sprigs fresh dill for every 2 cups (500 mL) gin in an airtight container. Leave for 3 to 4 days, shaking every day, then strain the radish and dill from the gin and discard. You will be left with a beautiful aromatic and spicy spirit. (See pages 193–4 for more detailed instructions.)

Muddling fresh herbs like thyme or rosemary in with the radish-infused spirit in this Caesar works well to add herbaceous flavour. The addition of muddled cucumber will bring coolness to this drink; citrus wedges will brighten the existing flavours.

Beetroot Caesar

· ·

Beets are a staple root vegetable of Canada, and you can find them on tables all across the country during family dinners. Although cooked beets are also tasty, this recipe uses the pickled kind. Whether you use store-bought pickled beets or your own homemade version, this recipe is sure to please all beet lovers.

Glass

Rim   Celery salt or Mott's Clamato Rimmer

What   3 1-inch (2.5 cm) chunks pickled beet
2 dashes cayenne hot sauce
2 dashes Worcestershire sauce
4 grinds fresh cracked black pepper
1 oz (30 mL) gin
4 oz (120 mL) Mott's Clamato Cocktail

Garnish   Pickled beets on a skewer

How   1. In a mixing glass, muddle everything but the gin and Mott's Clamato Cocktail.
2. Add the gin and Mott's Clamato Cocktail, and stir well to mix and spread the flavours around.
3. Rim a highball glass and fill to the top with ice.
4. Strain the mixture into the highball glass, and garnish.

· ·

Add a spoonful of horseradish for a different kind of heat, or garnish with fresh chives for a savoury scent.

Father's Day Caesar

Mother's Day Caesar and
Berry Cheesecake in a Jar
(recipe page 185)

Mother's Day Caesar

Flowers are always a popular gift on Mother's Day and here the classic rose, which is edible, is brought together with the Caesar taste. Pick up some rose-water and wow your mom with a drink to celebrate her day. Also feel free to go really big on the garnish and treat her to a day at the spa.

Glass

Rim   Fresh cracked salt and
              black pepper

What   1 oz (30 mL) vodka
              1 oz (30 mL) rosewater
              2 dashes Worcestershire sauce
              2 grinds fresh cracked
              black pepper
              3 oz (90 mL) Mott's Clamato
              Cocktail

Garnish   A single rose

How   1. Rim a highball glass with
              citrus and rimmer.
              2. Fill the glass to the top
              with ice.
              3. Add the ingredients in the
              order listed.
              4. Stir well to mix the cocktail,
              and garnish.

Quite a few floral flavours work well in this Caesar—hibiscus water, orange blossom water, and jasmine water are just some that can substitute for the rosewater, depending on your mom's taste.

Father's Day Caesar

Instead of getting your dad a new tie, whip up this tasty version of the Caesar, made with Scotch and beer. It's easy to make, and simple to serve in a pint glass. Garnish with a beautifully cooked steak dinner after a round of golf.

Glass

Rim   Celery salt or Mott's Clamato
              Rimmer

What   1 oz (30 mL) Scotch whisky
              2 dashes cayenne
              hot sauce
              2 dashes Worcestershire
              sauce
              2 grinds fresh cracked
              black pepper
              12 oz (355 mL) lager
              3 oz (90 mL) Mott's Clamato
              Cocktail

Garnish   Lime wedge

How   1. Rim a pint glass or beer
              mug with citrus and rimmer.
              2. Fill the glass to the top
              with ice.
              3. Add the ingredients in the
              order listed.
              4. Stir well to mix the cocktail,
              and garnish.

SUM

Ah, the long, lazy days of summer. The season of backyard BBQs, weekends by the water, relaxing, and recharging. Gardens and farm fields are in full bloom, offering a bounty of fresh, local ingredients. In this chapter, we'll help you beat the heat

MER

with no-sweat summertime Caesars, whether spiked with cool muddled cucumber or bursting with the refreshing combination of pineapple and basil. Savour the flavours of summer from Canada Day through to Labour Day.

Cucumber-Infused Caesar

. . . .

Nothing adds coolness and freshness to a cocktail like cucumber, and I find it makes a great counterpoint to the savoury nature of the Caesar. It's essential to muddle the cucumber slices right in the mixing glass, as you would with lime if making a Mojito. It takes a bit more effort, but it's well, well worth it.

Glass

Rim   Fresh cracked salt and black pepper

What   4 slices cucumber
           2 dashes Tabasco pepper sauce
           3 grinds fresh cracked salt and black pepper
           1 oz (30 mL) gin
           4 oz (120 mL) Mott's Clamato Cocktail

Garnish   Cucumber slice
           Fresh cracked salt and black pepper

How   1. In a mixing glass, muddle everything but the gin and
              Mott's Clamato Cocktail.
           2. Add the gin and Mott's Clamato Cocktail, and stir well
              to mix and spread the flavours around.
           3. Rim a highball glass and fill to the top with ice.
           4. Strain the mixture into the highball glass, and garnish.

. . . .

Add fresh basil, dill, or even mint to the muddle of ingredients for some herbiness. If you can find a cucumber-infused gin to use, even better, as it will lend another layer of cucumber flavour.

Thai Mango Caesar

· ·

Mixing fruit juices into a Caesar is great for people who don't like the taste of more traditional Caesars, as it sweetens the Mott's Clamato Cocktail. The other barrier to cross with non-Caesar fans is texture, and mango helps ease people's minds, as it has a thicker mouthfeel, similar to tomato juice. This recipe calls for Sriracha, a popular Thai hot sauce. This Caesar is one of my favourites to make for other people, and it always, always gets a hugely positive response.

Glass

Rim Fresh cracked salt and black pepper

What 1 oz (30 mL) white rum
½ barspoon Sriracha hot sauce
2 grinds fresh cracked black pepper
1½ oz (45 mL) mango nectar
2½ oz (75 mL) Mott's Clamato Cocktail

Garnish Mango chicken chunks on a skewer (or just mango chunks for ease)

How
1. Rim a highball glass with citrus and rimmer.
2. Fill the glass to the top with ice.
3. Add the ingredients in the order listed.
4. Stir well to mix the cocktail, and garnish.

· ·

The flavour of mango pairs well with many different and diverse ingredients, so it's fun to experiment. A rimmer of lemon pepper seasoning always brightens the mango flavour of the drink.

Peachy-Keen Caesar

· ·

This recipe was created as part of my quest to use every possible fruit in a Caesar! It's another great option for those who don't like the more classic versions, as the peach nectar is vibrant and bright and complements the savouriness of the Mott's Clamato Cocktail. The bitters help unite the flavours. I then bump it up a bit with Thai chili hot sauce to add a nice kick.

Glass

Rim   Fresh salt and pepper with toasted citrus zest

What
1 oz (30 mL) 100% blue agave tequila
1 oz (30 mL) peach nectar
¼ barspoon Thai chili hot sauce
1 dash Angostura bitters
3 grinds fresh cracked salt and black pepper
4 oz (120 mL) Mott's Clamato Cocktail

Garnish   Peach slices dusted with fresh cracked salt and
black pepper

How
1. Rim a highball glass with citrus and rimmer.
2. Fill the glass to the top with ice.
3. Add the ingredients in the order listed.
4. Stir well to mix the cocktail, and garnish.

· ·

Have extra peaches but no peach nectar? Slice them up and
muddle them in, for that peachy flavour. Out of peaches?
Nectarines or apricots can fill the gap.

Pineapple Basil Caesar

. . . .

The sweetness of pineapple, spiciness of tequila, and herbiness of basil all have one thing in common: they work well with pepper. Pepper is the key to this drink, and the basil, tequila, and cracked black pepper rim combine to create a trifecta of pepper in your mouth!

Glass

Rim Fresh cracked salt and black pepper

What 4 1-inch (2.5 cm) chunks fresh pineapple
4 fresh basil leaves, torn up
2 dashes jalapeño hot sauce
2 dashes Worcestershire sauce
5 grinds fresh cracked black pepper
1 oz (30 mL) 100% blue agave tequila
4 oz (120 mL) Mott's Clamato Cocktail

Garnish Pineapple chunks dipped in the rimmer, on a skewer
Fresh basil leaves

How 1. In a mixing glass, muddle everything but the tequila and Mott's Clamato Cocktail.
2. Add the tequila and Mott's Clamato Cocktail, and stir well to mix and spread the flavours around.
3. Rim a highball glass and fill to the top with ice.
4. Strain the mixture into the highball glass, and garnish.

. . . .

To make the easy version of this recipe, use pineapple juice instead of fresh chunks and omit the basil, just placing some chopped fresh leaves on top for garnish. Pineapple is a very versatile flavour, so for this drink have fun finding new pairings that are maybe a little bit out-there! Smoky flavours can be a great accent to pineapples, whether in the form of liquid smoke or a smoky whisky.

BBQ Corn Caesar

. . . .

Nothing says summer like BBQ corn on the cob. I shave the kernels right off the grilled corn and then muddle them with liquid smoke and lime wedges. Check your local grocer for liquid smoke. It usually comes in a hickory flavour and is an easy way to introduce a touch of smoki- ness to your food and drinks.

Glass

Rim   Fresh cracked salt and black pepper

What   3 barspoons BBQ corn kernels
4 dashes Worcestershire sauce
2 dashes jalapeño hot sauce
2 dashes liquid smoke
3 grinds fresh cracked black pepper
2 lime wedges
1 oz (30 mL) whisky
4 oz (120 mL) Mott's Clamato Cocktail

Garnish   BBQ corn on the cob, on a skewer

How   1. In a mixing glass, muddle everything but the whisky and Mott's Clamato Cocktail.
2. Add the whisky and Mott's Clamato Cocktail, and stir well to mix and spread the flavours around.
3. Rim a highball glass and fill to the top with ice.
4. Strain the mixture into the highball glass, and garnish.

Caesar Fresa

· ·

With the classic salsa elements of cilantro, onion, and lime, you've almost got a glass of pico de gallo with this Caesar! I continued with the Mexican vibe by adding a tequila base. The idea for this recipe came from a strawberry salsa, and the strawberries here add a sweet but tart hit, making this Caesar perfect for summer sipping.

Glass

Rim   Fresh cracked salt and black pepper

What   3 strawberries, stems removed
            2 lime wedges
            ½ jalapeño pepper (seeds optional for extra heat)
            2 sprigs fresh cilantro
            6 grinds fresh cracked black pepper
            1 oz (30 mL) 100% blue agave tequila
            4 oz (120 mL) Mott's Clamato Cocktail

Garnish Strawberry
             Lime wheel
             Sprig fresh cilantro

How   1. In a mixing glass, muddle everything but the tequila
               and Mott's Clamato Cocktail.
            2. Add the tequila and Mott's Clamato Cocktail, and stir
               well to mix and spread the flavours around.
            3. Rim a highball glass and fill to the top with ice.
            4. Strain the mixture into the highball glass, and garnish.

· ·

Strawberries pair well with lots of savoury flavours. Mix up this recipe by replacing the cilantro with ingredients like rhubarb or ginger, for a more sour or spicy note.

Jamaican Jerk Caesar

. . . .

Jerk spices work really well with tomatoes and, combined with Jamaican rum, this Caesar is a one-sip trip to the Caribbean! The next time you're serving jerk chicken at home, cut up some chunks, skewer them, and serve with this delicious Caesar recipe.

Glass

Rim Celery salt with jerk seasoning

What 1 oz (30 mL) Jamaican amber rum
     2 barspoons Jamaican jerk sauce
     3 dashes Worcestershire sauce
     2 dashes Scotch bonnet hot sauce
     3 grinds fresh cracked black pepper
     4 oz (120 mL) Mott's Clamato Cocktail

Garnish Jerk chicken on a skewer (or pineapple chunks for ease)

How 1. Rim a highball glass with citrus and rimmer.
     2. Fill the glass to the top with ice.
     3. Add the ingredients in the order listed.
     4. Stir well to mix the cocktail, and garnish.

. . . .

Spice this Caesar as desired, as everyone has a preferred level of heat. For a sweet twist, add citrus or even pineapple juice. This recipe also works with Cajun seasoning instead of the jerk, giving it a more Creole, blackened flavour profile.

Scotch bonnet peppers are synonymous with the Caribbean and commonly used in Jamaican cuisine, espcially in the form of hot sauce. This recipe will work just fine with less spicy hot sauces or even with an extremely spicy one.

Fireworks Caesar

. . . .

This Caesar is all about heat! It starts with a spicy spirit, tequila, that's then topped with garlic, jalapeño—remove the seeds if you want to keep the heat down, or leave them in and fire it up—and green onion. Muddle the mixture gooood and . . . KA-BOOM!

Glass

Rim   Celery salt with cayenne pepper

What   3 dashes HYH hot sauce (see page 9)
         2 grinds fresh cracked salt and black pepper
         ½ jalapeño pepper (seeds optional for extra heat)
         1 garlic clove, minced
         ½ green onion
         1 oz (30 mL) 100% blue agave tequila
         4 oz (120 mL) Mott's Clamato Cocktail

Garnish Spicy prawn on a skewer

How   1. In a mixing glass, muddle everything but the tequila
            and Mott's Clamato Cocktail.
         2. Add the tequila and Mott's Clamato Cocktail, and stir
            well to mix and spread the flavours around.
         3. Rim a highball glass and fill to the top with ice.
         4. Strain the mixture into the highball glass, and garnish.

. . . .

To up the ante on the spice in this Caesar, use a chili pepper–infused spirit in place of the tequila. Love spicy shrimp? The next time you're cooking them up at home, throw some on top of this Caesar, for another spicy treat.

Blueberry Caesar

· ·

Blueberries can be found all over this great country and are used in plenty of food dishes, both sweet and savoury. This Caesar combines blueberries with a classic brandy liqueur, Grand Marnier. Although both ingredients are sweet, the addition of fresh cracked black pepper brings a savouriness to this Caesar that is unique. Add some Canadian cheese curds to the garnish of pepper-dusted blueberries and you're sure to be pleasantly surprised.

Glass

Rim Fresh cracked salt and black pepper with
     ground dried blueberries

What ½ oz (15 mL) fresh lemon juice
      2 dashes jalapeño hot sauce
      2 dashes Angostura bitters
      4 grinds fresh cracked black pepper
      6 blueberries
      1 oz (30 mL) Grand Marnier
      3 oz (90 mL) Mott's Clamato Cocktail

Garnish Black pepper–dusted blueberries and cheese curds
         on a skewer

How 1. In a mixing glass, muddle everything but the Grand
        Marnier and Mott's Clamato Cocktail.
     2. Add the Grand Marnier and Mott's Clamato Cocktail,
        and stir well to mix and spread the flavours around.
     3. Rim a highball glass and fill to the top with ice.
     4. Strain the mixture into the highball glass, and garnish.

· ·

If you are unable to find Grand Marnier, there are
many other orange-flavoured spirits to choose from, including
Cointreau, Triple Sec, and orange Curaçao.

Lobster Caesar

· ·

Canadian lobster is among the best in the world. The next time you're having friends over for a good old-fashioned lobster boil, whip up some of these Caesars to complement the seafood, and don't forget to take your garnish over the top. They are sure to be wowed with a lobster tail sticking out of the glass!

Glass

Rim   Celery salt with fresh cracked black pepper

What   1 oz (30 mL) lobster broth
3 dashes hot sauce
2 dashes Worcestershire sauce
3 sprigs fresh dill
1 oz (30 mL) gin
3 oz (90 mL) Mott's Clamato Cocktail

Garnish Poached lobster tail on a skewer
Sprig fresh dill

How   1. In a mixing glass, muddle everything but the gin and Mott's Clamato Cocktail.
2. Add the gin and Mott's Clamato Cocktail, and stir well to mix and spread the flavours around.
3. Rim a highball glass and fill to the top with ice.
4. Strain the mixture into the highball glass, and garnish.

· ·

If you're not a fan of dill, use other fresh herbs,
like cilantro, basil, or even mint.

Stampede Caesar

The Calgary Stampede is a world-famous Canadian summertime tradition. Rye whisky is a staple spirit in Alberta, and the province's legendary beef is a mainstay on any menu. Beef up this Caesar with beef stock (a must-have ingredient for this one), a piece of AAA Alberta beef on a skewer for garnish, and a steak spice rimmer on the glass. It's time to say "Howdy, partner!"

Glass

Rim   Fresh cracked salt and black pepper with steak spice

What   1 oz (30 mL) Alberta premium rye whisky
         4 dashes Worcestershire sauce
         2 dashes hot sauce
         3 pinches steak spice
         3 grinds fresh cracked salt and black pepper
         1 oz (30 mL) beef stock
         3 oz (90 mL) Mott's Clamato Cocktail

Garnish Grilled Alberta flank steak on a skewer

How   1. Rim a highball glass with citrus and rimmer.
         2. Fill the glass to the top with ice.
         3. Add the ingredients in the order listed.
         4. Stir well to mix the cocktail, and garnish.

Chelada Caesar

Lazy Long-Weekend Caesar

Sea-Salt Pretzel Bites
with Beer Cheese Dip
(recipe page 151)

Lazy Long-Weekend Caesar

Long weekends are all about kicking back and relaxing. Just grab a Mott's Clamato Ready-to-Drink Caesar Original and pour it into a glass over ice. A splash of fresh juice will add a refreshing zing to beat the heat.

Glass

Rim   Celery salt or Mott's Clamato Rimmer (optional)

What   1 can or bottle Mott's Clamato Ready-to-Drink Caesar Original (about 12 oz/ 355 mL)
          2 oz (60 mL) fresh orange juice

Garnish   Whatever's on the BBQ, skewer it and use it!

How   1. Rim a highball glass with citrus and rimmer.
          2. Fill the glass to the top with ice.
          3. Add the ingredients in the order listed.
          4. Stir well to mix the cocktail, and garnish.

Orange juice is probably the easiest to grab from the fridge, but other juices, like mango or pineapple, work just as well.

Chelada Caesar

In Canada we sometimes call the mixture of Mott's Clamato Cocktail and beer a Beezer; in the southern United States and Mexico, it's Chelada. Either way, it's easy to prepare and tastes delicious!

Glass

Rim   None

What   12 oz (355 mL) your favourite beer
          3 dashes jalapeño hot sauce (optional)
          2 dashes Worcestershire sauce (optional)
          4 oz (120 mL) Mott's Clamato Cocktail

Garnish   None

How   1. Pour the beer into a pint glass or beer mug, then add the Mott's Clamato Cocktail.

We all have our own perfect ratio of beer to Mott's Clamato Cocktail. Play around with the proportions to find what works best for you. Try spicing this drink by adding hot sauce and/or Worcestershire sauce.

Strawberry Daiquiri Caesar

Margarita Caesar

Piña Colada Caesar

Strawberry Daiquiri Caesar

· ·

We love our Caesars extra cold, so why not take it to the extreme and make them frozen? Strawberries, basil, and rum are balanced by the hints of savoury and spice in this deliciously slushy concoction.

Glass

Rim   Fresh cracked salt and black pepper

What 2 oz (30 mL) rum
3 dashes hot sauce
5 grinds fresh cracked salt and black pepper
4 fresh basil leaves, finely chopped
2 oz (60 mL) Mr & Mrs T* Strawberry
   Daiquiri mix
2 oz (60 mL) fresh lime juice
4 oz (120 mL) Mott's Clamato Cocktail

Garnish Lime wheels
Fresh cracked black pepper

How   1. Place all the ingredients in a blender.
2. Add an equal amount of crushed or broken-up ice.
3. Blend until smooth.
4. Pour into a hurricane glass, and garnish.

· ·

Adding Worcestershire sauce to this frozen Caesar is optional, as it will dramatically change the taste. Add it if you prefer a saltier taste, or leave it out for a more savoury flavour.

If you are unable to find a premade strawberry daiquiri mix, you can easily substitute with 5 or 6 fresh strawberries, stems removed.

Margarita Caesar

· ·

The margarita is one of summer's most popular frozen cocktails, and this recipe combines the classic mix of tequila and lime with the Caesar. This recipe is kept simple, but it can easily be ramped up by adding finely chopped herbs like mint or basil to the blender. Have fun getting creative with your new frozen Caesar concoction.

Glass

Rim   Fresh cracked salt and black pepper

What   2 oz (60 mL) 100% blue agave tequila
              3 dashes jalapeño hot sauce
              5 grinds fresh cracked salt and black pepper
              4 oz (120 mL) Mr & Mrs T Margarita mix
              4 oz (120 mL) Mott's Clamato Cocktail

Garnish   Lime wheel

How   1. Place all the ingredients in a blender.
              2. Add an equal amount of crushed or broken-up ice.
              3. Blend until smooth.
              4. Pour into a margarita glass, and garnish.

· ·

Any bar lime mix can easily be substituted for the margarita mix, or you can even make it fresh using 2 cups (500 mL) freshly squeezed lemon or lime juice with 1 cup (250 mL) simple syrup. To make simple syrup, add 1 cup (250 mL) granulated sugar to 1 cup (250 mL) water in a saucepan set over medium heat, and stir until the sugar is completely dissolved. Let cool before using.

Piña Colada Caesar

· ·

Piña Colada and Caesar, two classic cocktails, are married here for an overwhelmingly delicious frozen drink! A number of food dishes combine coconut and tomatoes, but few drinks do. This cocktail really shows off this unique flavour combination.

Glass

Rim   Fresh cracked salt and black pepper

What   2 oz (60 mL) rum
              3 dashes cayenne hot sauce
              5 grinds fresh cracked salt and black pepper
              4 oz (120 mL) Mr & Mrs T Piña Colada mix
              4 oz (120 mL) Mott's Clamato Cocktail

Garnish   Lime wedge

How   1. Place all the ingredients in a blender.
              2. Add an equal amount of crushed or broken-up ice.
              3. Blend until smooth.
              4. Pour into a hurricane glass, and garnish.

FA

Fall always makes me think of crisp leaves and brisk mornings, with a hint of woodsmoke in the air. In this chapter you'll find Caesars imbued with the flavours of fall—apples, sage, roasted

LL

peppers, and artichokes. You'll also find plenty of occasion-specific Caesars perfect for your Thanksgiving and Halloween celebrations.

Thanksgiving Caesar

· ·

Show your friends how thankful you are for them by offering up this serve-yourself Caesar punch. This is a great way to keep your guests' glasses filled throughout the festivities. Let us give thanks for the Caesar—and for this extra-easy holiday entertaining method.

Glass

Rim   Fresh cracked salt and black pepper

What   3 cups (750 mL) whisky
4 cups (1 L) apple cider or juice
4 cups (1 L) Mott's Clamato Cocktail
Hot sauce, to taste
Worcestershire sauce, to taste
Fresh cracked salt and black pepper, to taste

Garnish Lemon and lime wheels
Cinnamon sticks
DIY garnish bar (see Tip)

How   1. Set up stations with glasses and the rimmer, ice and punch, and garnish.
2. Fill the punch bowl with the ingredients and stir well.
3. Explain to guests the steps to make their drinks: Rim. Ice. Pour. Garnish.

· ·

Tip: Having a DIY garnish bar makes this self-serve set-up amazing. Spread out your favourite Caesar garnishes—fruit, cheese, pickles, olives, shrimp, or charcuterie—for your guests to choose from (see photo on page 5). And don't forget, they can double as snacks or hors d'oeuvres! Lemon and lime wheels and cinnamon sticks are perfect for the punch bowl.

Whisky & Sage Caesar

. . . .

Here's another great Caesar for Thanksgiving, made with Canadian whisky. The sage adds a soft savoury flavour, and since it's a common ingredient for seasoning turkey, it gives this cocktail a comfort-food, holiday-dinner vibe.

Glass

Rim   Fresh cracked salt and black pepper

What   6 fresh sage leaves
2 dashes hot sauce
2 dashes Angostura bitters
1 oz (30 mL) Canadian whisky
4 oz (120 mL) Mott's Clamato Cocktail

Garnish   Fresh sage leaves

How
1. In a mixing glass, muddle everything but the whisky and Mott's Clamato Cocktail.
2. Add the whisky and Mott's Clamato Cocktail, and stir well to mix and spread the flavours around.
3. Rim a highball glass and fill to the top with ice.
4. Strain the mixture into the highball glass, and garnish.

. . . .

Thyme and rosemary are two other popular herbs you could use along with the sage, or you could grind up some spices like clove or even anise and add them to the rimmer.

Sweet Chili Heat Caesar

· ·

The amazing array of flavours and tastes from all over the world is one of the great things about Canada's multicultural mosaic. Sweet chili sauce (typically used in Thai food) is almost as popular as BBQ or hot sauce. It's likely that you have some sweet chili sauce at home, so why not use it in a Caesar? Combined with rum and spicy Sriracha hot sauce, it makes one delicious sweet/heat-balanced drink.

Glass

Rim Fresh cracked salt and black pepper

What 1 oz (30 mL) white rum
1 tbsp (5 mL) sweet chili sauce
½ barspoon Sriracha hot sauce
1 dash Worcestershire sauce
3 grinds fresh cracked salt and black pepper
4 oz (120 mL) Mott's Clamato Cocktail

Garnish Fresh cracked black pepper

How
1. Rim a highball glass with citrus and rimmer.
2. Fill the glass to the top with ice.
3. Add the ingredients in the order listed.
4. Stir well to mix the cocktail, and garnish.

· ·

Unusual herbs like Thai basil or lemon verbena muddled into this drink can bring something fun to the flavour party, both to the nose and to the taste buds. And if you're serving Thai food when making this, add a sweet-chili chicken skewer, for the ultimate garnish.

Maple BBQ Caesar

· ·

Canadian whisky and maple BBQ sauce—if you're looking for a great cooler-weather Caesar, here you go!

Glass

Rim Montreal steak spice

What 1 oz (30 mL) Canadian whisky
1 tsp (5 mL) maple-flavoured BBQ sauce
3 dashes Worcestershire sauce
2 dashes hot sauce
3 grinds fresh cracked salt and black pepper
4 oz (120 mL) Mott's Clamato Cocktail

Garnish Knot of maple bacon on a skewer
Fresh cracked black pepper

How 1. Rim a highball glass with citrus and rimmer.
2. Fill the glass to the top with ice.
3. Add the ingredients in the order listed.
4. Stir well to mix the cocktail, and garnish.

· ·

If you don't have maple-flavoured BBQ sauce, it's quite all right; any other BBQ sauce will do the trick. To make the sauce easier to mix into the Caesar, thin it by diluting it with juice—orange, apple, or mango, say—or with my personal favourite, whisky!

Bacon bits, whether store-bought or homemade, make a great addition to this Caesar's rimmer. Just run the bits through a coffee grinder or food processor and add to the steak spice rim. And knots of maple bacon—strips of raw bacon tied in knots and then cooked in a frying pan or in the oven on parchment paper and slathered with maple BBQ sauce—make just about the best garnish for this Caesar I can think of.

Oktoberfest Caesar

. . . .

Oktoberfest is German in heritage but celebrated heartily right across Canada. Here's a perfect Caesar for the fest, featuring a distinctive German flavour, sauerkraut, which is right at home in Canada's cocktail.

Glass

Rim   Fresh cracked salt and black pepper

What   1 oz (30 mL) Canadian whisky
3 dashes hot sauce
2 dashes Worcestershire sauce
5 grinds fresh cracked black pepper
4 oz (120 mL) Mott's Clamato Cocktail
1 barspoon sauerkraut

Garnish Sauerkraut
Oktoberfest sausage on a skewer

How   1. Rim a highball glass with citrus and rimmer.
2. Fill the glass to the top with ice.
3. Add the ingredients in the order listed.
4. Stir well to mix the cocktail, and garnish.

. . . .

This recipe works great with any sausage you're having for dinner. Whether you're frying it up in a pan or grilling it as part of a late fall BBQ, skewer some sausage to garnish your Caesar with! Kimchi is a great substitute for the sauerkraut.

West Coast Caesar

. . . .

Any Caesar rimmer should either contrast or complement the drink. The one here is a contrast, as the Chinese five spice powder helps mellow the seafood flavours of the cocktail. I designed this Caesar using a British Columbia–made gin, added oyster sauce to reflect the wealth of seafood in BC, and capped it off with Sriracha hot sauce and a rim that includes Chinese five spice, to represent the diverse Vancouver culture.

Glass

Rim   Fresh cracked salt and black pepper with Chinese five spice powder

What   1 oz (30 mL) gin (preferably distilled in British Columbia)
½ barspoon Sriracha hot sauce
½ barspoon oyster sauce
3 dashes Worcestershire sauce
3 grinds fresh cracked salt and black pepper
4 oz (120 mL) Mott's Clamato Cocktail

Garnish   Plate of fresh BC oysters

How   1. Rim a highball glass with citrus and rimmer.
        2. Fill the glass to the top with ice.
        3. Add the ingredients in the order listed.
        4. Stir well to mix the cocktail, and garnish.

. . . .

If you're not an oyster fan, take home sushi from your local supermarket or sushi restaurant. Salmon or tuna rolls are a great complement to the oyster sauce in this Caesar.

Mediterranean Caesar

. . . .

Combining classic herbs, citrus flavours, balsamic vinegar, and salty capers, this Caesar conjures up the cuisine of the Mediterranean, with its sun-kissed shores.

Glass

Rim   Celery salt with lemon pepper seasoning

What
1 oz (30 mL) gin
1 barspoon capers, drained
Sprig each fresh thyme, rosemary, marjoram,
    or whatever's available
2 fresh sage leaves
2 barspoons balsamic vinegar
3 grinds fresh cracked salt and black pepper
½ oz (15 mL) fresh lemon juice
4 oz (120 mL) Mott's Clamato Cocktail

Garnish
Cherry tomatoes and cheese-stuffed olive on
    a skewer
Capers
Sprig of a fresh herb used in the Caesar, or a sprig of each

How
1. Rim a highball glass with citrus and rimmer.
2. Fill the glass to the top with ice.
3. Add the ingredients in the order listed.
4. Stir well to mix the cocktail, and garnish.

. . . .

If you love a briny, acidic taste to your Caesar, add a vinegar. There are many types that will mix things up. I use balsamic in this recipe, but you could also use red wine, sherry, or any one of the flavour-infused options available at the grocery store.

Black Cherry Caesar

. . . .

Cherries and tomatoes are an interesting flavour combination and work surprisingly well together. The smoky chipotle and lots of pepper add a nice heat to offset the sweetness of the fruit, and the hint of cinnamon and sugar in the rimmer help balance the sour and savoury flavours with a spicy yet sweet note.

Glass

Rim   Fresh cracked salt and black pepper with cinnamon and granulated sugar

What   4 pitted black cherries, stems removed
            3 dashes chipotle hot sauce
            2 dashes Worcestershire sauce
            5 grinds fresh cracked black pepper
            1 oz (30 mL) whisky
            3 oz (90 mL) Mott's Clamato Cocktail

Garnish Black cherry

How   1. In a mixing glass, muddle everything but the whisky and Mott's Clamato Cocktail.
            2. Add the whisky and Mott's Clamato Cocktail, and stir well to mix and spread the flavours around.
            3. Rim a highball glass and fill to the top with ice.
            4. Strain the mixture into the highball glass, and garnish.

. . . .

From muddling fresh cherries to adding flavoured soda, juice, or even cherry-infused spirits, there are plenty of ways to get even more cherry flavour into your Caesar.

Apple Shrub Caesar

. . . .

"Shrub" refers to cocktails that contain vinegar, and they've had a resurgence in popularity over the last couple of years, with more and more cocktail bars putting them on their menus. This recipe uses apple cider vinegar. The spiced rum adds sweetness to the mix, so you get a nice balance of flavours.

Glass

Rim   Montreal steak spice with ground anise

What 1 oz (30 mL) spiced rum
3 dashes Angostura bitters
2 dashes jalapeño hot sauce
1 dash Worcestershire sauce
Pinch Montreal steak spice
2 barspoons apple cider vinegar
1 oz (30 mL) apple cider or juice
4 oz (120 mL) Mott's Clamato Cocktail

Garnish Apple slice

How 1. Rim a highball glass with citrus and rimmer.
2. Fill the glass to the top with ice.
3. Add the ingredients in the order listed.
4. Stir well to mix the cocktail, and garnish.

. . . .

Wrapping bacon around the apple slice and sprinkling it with a little brown sugar before baking in the oven at 375°F (190°C) until brown is a great way to spruce up the garnish of this Caesar.

Roasted Red Pepper & Sun-Dried Tomato Caesar

. . . .

This Caesar combines the five tastes that your tongue can identify: sweet, salty, sour, bitter, and umami. Muddling the sweet smoky pepper, tangy sun-dried tomatoes, salty Worcestershire, and sour, bitter lime together makes for a mouth-watering balance.

Glass

Rim Fresh cracked salt and black pepper with chili flakes

What 3 1-inch (2.5 cm) squares roasted red bell pepper
3 sun-dried tomatoes, drained of oil
3 dashes Worcestershire sauce
2 dashes cayenne hot sauce
3 grinds fresh cracked salt and black pepper
2 lime wedges
1 oz (30 mL) gin
4 oz (120 mL) Mott's Clamato Cocktail

Garnish Grilled vegetables (red bell pepper, zucchini, tomatoes) on a skewer

How 1. In a mixing glass, muddle everything but the gin and Mott's Clamato Cocktail.
2. Add the gin and Mott's Clamato Cocktail, and stir well to mix and spread the flavours around.
3. Rim a highball glass and fill to the top with ice.
4. Strain the mixture into the highball glass, and garnish.

Kai-Saru Caesar

. . . .

Kai-Saru is the traditional Japanese pronunciation of the word Caesar (or, in Japanese, シーザー), and this recipe is a special tribute to the wonderful flavours Japanese cuisine has given to the world. Sake is the base, layered with the delicate acidity of rice vinegar, pickled ginger juice, and soy sauce, and capped off with some heat from the wasabi. Finally, while not mandatory, garnishing this baby with a battered clam sushi roll makes it a cross-cultural work of art.

Glass

Rim   Fresh cracked salt and black pepper

What   1½ oz (45 mL) sake
1/4 oz (7.5 mL) rice vinegar
1/4 oz (7.5 mL) pickled ginger juice
½ oz (15 mL) soy sauce
½ barspoon wasabi paste
3 grinds fresh cracked black pepper
3 oz (90 mL) Mott's Clamato Cocktail

Garnish   Your favourite kind of sushi roll

How   1. Rim a rocks glass with citrus and rimmer.
2. Fill the glass to the top with ice.
3. Add the ingredients in the order listed.
4. Stir well to mix the cocktail, and garnish.

. . . .

You could substitute Japanese whisky instead of sake;
just be aware that it will give you a bigger, stronger spirit taste.
There are so many other flavours from Japan that you could
also incorporate into a Caesar, like fish and oyster sauces or,
my favourite on rice, ponzu.

Mustard-Infused Caesar

· ·

Mustard is a classic condiment and tastes great in a Caesar. Getting the flavour into the drink and still making the drink look palatable can be a struggle, though, as the mustard tends to break up into little particles. I recommend infusing your favourite spirit with mustard, then using that spirit to make this tasty recipe.

Glass

Rim   Fresh cracked salt and black pepper

What   1 oz (30 mL) mustard-infused vodka (see pages 193–4)
             3 dashes Worcestershire sauce
             2 dashes jalapeño hot sauce
             3 pinches fresh cracked black pepper
             ½ oz (15 mL) pickle brine
             4 oz (120 mL) Mott's Clamato Cocktail

Garnish Mustard-laden sliced meat on a skewer

How   1. Rim a highball glass with citrus and rimmer.
             2. Fill the glass to the top with ice.
             3. Add the ingredients in the order listed.
             4. Stir well to mix the cocktail, and garnish.

· ·

All types of mustard can be infused into alcohols, including into tequila and whisky. To up the mustard quotient, add mustard pickles to the garnish.

Artichoke Caesar

· ·

If you like artichokes, you're going to love this recipe. It's based on a classic Italian bitter liqueur called Cynar (pronounced "CHEE-nar"), and is flavoured with various herbs and plants, most notably artichoke.

Glass

Rim   Fresh cracked salt and black pepper

What   ¼ pickled artichoke
             4 dashes Worcestershire sauce
             3 dashes hot sauce
             4 grinds fresh cracked black pepper
             1 oz (30 mL) gin
             ½ oz (15 mL) Cynar
             3 oz (90 mL) Mott's Clamato Cocktail

Garnish Artichoke chunks on a skewer
             Lime wedge

How   1. In a mixing glass, muddle everything but the gin,
                Cynar, and Mott's Clamato Cocktail.
             2. Add the gin, Cynar, and Mott's Clamato Cocktail, and
                stir well to mix and spread the flavours around.
             3. Rim a highball glass and fill to the top with ice.
             4. Strain the mixture into the highball glass, and garnish.

Halloween Caesar

Ghosts and jack-o'-lanterns are synonymous with Halloween, and this recipe integrates both themes of this fall celebration into one Caesar. Just beware of the ghost pepper if you're not a fan of heat, as this bad boy will be sure to make you sweat.

Glass

Rim   Montreal steak spice with pumpkin spice

What   1 oz (30 mL) rum
             3 dashes ghost pepper hot sauce
             2 dashes Worcestershire sauce
             3 grinds fresh cracked black pepper
             1 oz (30 mL) fresh blood orange juice
             3 oz (90 mL) Mott's Clamato Cocktail

Garnish Orange cut like a jack-o'-lantern

How   1. Rim a highball glass with citrus and rimmer.
             2. Fill the glass to the top with ice.
             3. Add the ingredients in the order listed.
             4. Stir well to mix the cocktail, and garnish.

**To prepare the garnish, slice off a large disc of orange peel.
Use a paring knife to cut out the eyes, nose, and mouth.**

Gin & Ginger Caesar

· ·

This is a Caesar spin on one of my other favourite cocktails, the Dark and Stormy. Instead of using dark rum, I've gone for gin, ginger beer, and, of course, Mott's Clamato Cocktail. It's simple, a little spicy, and very refreshing.

Glass

Rim   Fresh cracked salt and black pepper

What   1 oz (30 mL) ginger-infused gin (see pages 193–4)
             2 dashes hot sauce
             2 dashes Worcestershire sauce
             2 oz (60 mL) ginger beer
             2 oz (60 mL) Mott's Clamato Cocktail

Garnish Ginger prawn on a skewer (or candied ginger for ease)

How   1. Rim a highball glass with citrus and rimmer.
             2. Fill the glass to the top with ice.
             3. Add the ingredients in the order listed.
             4. Stir well to mix the cocktail, and garnish.

· ·

Ginger works great on its own and also as a complementing flavour. Using the juice from pickled ginger would add a nice bright acidic punch to this Caesar. Ginger is also often paired with seafood, so garnish this drink with your favourite— perhaps a prawn—for an interesting twist.

WIN

Welcome to winter, the season of friends, fire-side gatherings, and holiday celebrations. In this chapter, you'll find satisfyingly savoury Caesars hitting all the right notes to counter the chill of the season—Caesars with hot pickles,

TER

spicy pimento, and the ultimate comfort food of all, bacon! You'll also find tasty and tempting crowd-pleasers for holiday entertaining made simple and stress-free.

Hot Pickled Caesar

· ·

One thing that never changes for Caesar fans, regardless of where they live, is their love of sharing their "secret Caesar ingredient." The funny thing is, so many of us love the same thing: pickle brine! From classic dill or sweet-and-sour to your family recipe, pickle brine in Caesars always tastes amazing. Chances are you have a jar of pickles sitting in your refrigerator right now. Pair the brine with a hit of horseradish and you've just upped your Caesar game for good.

Glass

Rim   Celery salt or Mott's Clamato Rimmer

What   1 oz (30 mL) vodka
             4 dashes Worcestershire sauce
             2 dashes hot sauce
             3 pinches celery salt
             ½ barspoon extra-hot horseradish
             ½ oz (15 mL) pickle brine
             4 oz (120 mL) Mott's Clamato Cocktail

Garnish Dill pickle and cheese on a skewer

How   1. Rim a highball glass with citrus and rimmer.
             2. Fill the glass to the top with ice.
             3. Add the ingredients in the order listed.
             4. Stir well to mix the cocktail, and garnish.

· ·

To make the garnish, simply slice a baby dill pickle in half lengthwise. Then place a similar-sized slice of your favourite cheese in the middle of the two halves and secure with a toothpick. Enjoy!

**Avoid using creamy styles of horseradish,
as it will make your Caesar look milky.**

Bacon-ato

. . . .

Bacon, bacon, bacon! It really deserves to be a food group all on its own. I love bacon so much that I've added it to this Caesar in every possible way. Yummmm . . .

Glass

Rim   Ground bacon bits dusted with fresh cracked black pepper

What   1 oz (30 mL) bacon-infused spirit (see pages 193–4)
             3 dashes Worcestershire sauce
             2 dashes bacon-flavoured hot sauce
             5 grinds fresh cracked salt and black pepper
             4 oz (120 mL) Mott's Clamato Cocktail

Garnish Bacon!

How   1. Rim a highball glass with citrus and rimmer.
             2. Fill the glass to the top with ice.
             3. Add the ingredients in the order listed.
             4. Stir well to mix the cocktail, and garnish.

. . . .

There are many types and flavours of bacon to choose from—
peppered, smoked, maple, or even peameal—and any of them will
work in this recipe. And there are many ways to garnish with bacon,
from classic strips to knots, straws, or even full-on sandwiches!

Spicy Pimento Caesar

. . . .

Olive and pimento are a match made in heaven, but the pimento flavour is so often overshadowed by the olive. This Caesar uses the same flavour combination but gives the pimento the glory this time, as the spicy pimento paste is what really stands out when mixed together with gin and Mott's Clamato Cocktail.

Glass

Rim   Fresh cracked salt and black pepper

What   1 oz (30 mL) gin
2 dashes Worcestershire sauce
3 grinds fresh cracked black pepper
2 barspoons hot pimento paste
½ oz (15 mL) olive brine
3 oz (90 mL) Mott's Clamato Cocktail

Garnish Pimento-stuffed olives on a skewer

How   1. Rim a highball glass with citrus and rimmer.
2. Fill the glass to the top with ice.
3. Add the ingredients in the order listed.
4. Stir well to mix the cocktail, and garnish.

. . . .

Muddling a few olives with the gin and pickle brine is a great way to boost the classic-cocktail flavour combination. You can also introduce another salty flavour by adding capers.

Lord Stanley's Caesar

Don Cherry Caesar

Lord Stanley's Caesar

This recipe is a nod to hockey's championship trophy. We use gin and Scotch, as both would likely be found in Lord Stanley's liquor cabinet. The perfect vessel to serve it in would, of course, be the Cup itself.

Glass

Rim Fresh cracked salt
        and black pepper

What 1 oz (30 mL) gin
        4 dashes hot sauce
        2 dashes Angostura bitters
        ¼ oz (7.5 mL) pickle brine
        4 oz (120 mL) Mott's Clamato
        Cocktail
        Float smoky Scotch whisky

Garnish Pickled beans or
        asparagus

How 1. Rim a highball glass with
        citrus and rimmer.
        2. Fill the glass to the top
        with ice.
        3. Add the ingredients in the
        order listed, except for the
        whisky.
        4. Stir well to mix the cocktail,
        float the whisky, and
        garnish.

. . . .

**For those who want to celebrate
with bubbly, float a little inexpensive
champagne or sparkling wine on top
instead of the whisky.**

Don Cherry Caesar

Hockey's favourite commentator surely deserves his own version of Canada's cocktail. With Grapes as his nickname, I had to include a bit of grape juice—and fine Canadian pilsner for his dog, Blue.

Glass

Rim None

What 2 dashes jalapeño hot sauce
        3 grinds fresh cracked salt
        and black pepper
        2 oz (60 mL) grape juice
        6 oz (180 mL) pilsner
        6 oz (180 mL) Mott's
        Clamato Cocktail

Garnish 2 green grapes, on the
        stem
        Lime wedge

How 1. Add the ingredients to a pint
        glass or beer mug in the
        order listed.

. . . .

**Your choice of white or red grape juice
for this recipe will have more of an
effect on colour than it will on taste.**

Smoked-Out Caesar

. . . .

Smoke is one of the flavours many people enjoy in their Caesar, and this recipe offers plenty of ways you can add smoky flavour. Between the chipotle hot sauce, liquid smoke, and smoked paprika, this Caesar gives you more smoke than a forest fire! These smoky elements work great together or on their own, if you want to add them individually to other recipes.

Glass

Rim   Fresh cracked salt and black pepper with bacon bits
              and smoked paprika

What   1 oz (30 mL) peat-smoke Scotch whisky
              3 dashes chipotle hot sauce
              2 dashes Angostura bitters
              2 dashes liquid smoke
              2 dashes Worcestershire sauce
              4 oz (120 mL) Mott's Clamato Cocktail

Garnish Smoked Gouda cheese wrapped in Montreal smoked meat,
              on a skewer

How   1. Rim a highball glass with citrus and rimmer.
              2. Fill the glass to the top with ice.
              3. Add the ingredients in the order listed.
              4. Stir well to mix the cocktail, and garnish.

. . . .

Have fun incorporating any other smoky-flavoured ingredients into this recipe, like pulled pork jerky or even smoked salmon.

'Tis the Season to Caesar

Just like the Thanksgiving Caesar, this is a do-it-yourself for your guests, perfect for when entertaining during the holiday season. Pull out the punch bowl and set up the various stations and let your friends go at it and have fun!

Glass

Rim   Celery salt or Mott's Clamato Rimmer

What   3 cups (750 mL) vodka or gin
             7 cups (1.89 L) Mott's Clamato The Works
             2 cups (500 mL) cranberry juice
             Hot sauce, to taste
             Worcestershire sauce, to taste
             Fresh cracked salt and black pepper, to taste

Garnish Lemon and lime wheels
             Cranberries
             DIY garnish bar (see tip on page 80)

How   1. Set up stations with glasses and the rimmer, ice and punch, and garnish.
             2. Fill the punch bowl with the ingredients and stir well.
             3. Explain to guests the steps to make their drinks: Rim. Ice. Pour. Garnish.

Mott's Clamato The Works contains a balanced blend of seasonings, extra spices, and peppers along with the flavour and heat of horseradish; feel free to make it your own version by adding your favourite blend of herbs and spices.

Social Caesar

. . . .

Having friends over or throwing a party? This easy-to-make punch is easy
to prepare for any event, from winter backyard BBQs to TV viewing on
game day, and you get to double your garnishes as appetizers or snacks!

Glass

Rim   Celery salt or Mott's Clamato Rimmer

What   3 cups (750 mL) vodka or other spirit
7 cups (1.89 L) Mott's Clamato The Works

Garnish DIY garnish bar (see Tip)

How
1. Set up stations with glasses and the rimmer, ice and punch, and garnish.
2. Fill the punch bowl with the ingredients and stir well.
3. Explain to guests the steps to make their drinks: Rim. Ice. Pour. Garnish.

. . . .

**Lemons and limes can add a punch of colour to your bowl
of punch, and some fresh grated horseradish can be
refreshing to the eyes, nose, and tongue.**

**Tip: Create a DIY garnish bar for your guests to choose from,
for an amazing self-serve set-up. Basic meats, cheeses, and
pickles are always nice. Maybe step it up on game day to
chicken wings or mini burgers—it's completely up to you!**

see photo
overleaf

Warm Cerignola Olives with Fennel & Lemon
(recipe page 143)

Social Caesar

Pomegranate Caesar

. . . .

Pomegranate juice pairs well with the other flavours in this Caesar, including the chipotle and, of course, Mott's Clamato Cocktail. It also adds a great, rich colour that gives visual pop.

Glass

Rim Fresh cracked salt and black pepper

What 1 oz (30 mL) 100% blue agave tequila
½ oz (15 mL) fresh lemon juice
2 dashes chipotle hot sauce
1 dash Worcestershire sauce
3 grinds fresh cracked salt and black pepper
1 oz (30 mL) pomegranate juice
3 oz (90 mL) Mott's Clamato Cocktail

Garnish Pomegranate seeds
Sprig fresh cilantro

How 1. Rim a highball glass with citrus and rimmer.
2. Fill the glass to the top with ice.
3. Add the ingredients in the order listed.
4. Stir well to mix the cocktail, and garnish.

French Toast Pie with
Warm Maple Syrup
(recipe page 186)

Pomegranate Caesar

My Darling Clementine Caesar
(recipe page 128)

My Darling Clementine Caesar

. . . .

Despite their sunny freshness, clementines always make me think of winter—that's when we Canadians find boxes of them stacked up in the grocery store just waiting for us to take them home. The muddled fruit and orange blossom water in this recipe add a beautiful but subtle fruitiness.

Glass

Rim   Fresh cracked salt and black pepper

What   ½ peeled clementine
½ oz (15 mL) orange blossom water
2 dashes Tabasco hot sauce
1 dash Worcestershire sauce
4 grinds fresh cracked black pepper
1 oz (30 mL) gin
4 oz (120 mL) Mott's Clamato Cocktail

Garnish   Lime twist
Clementine segments

How
1. In a mixing glass, muddle everything but the gin and Mott's Clamato Cocktail.
2. Add the gin and Mott's Clamato Cocktail, and stir well to mix and spread the flavours around.
3. Rim a highball glass and fill to the top with ice.
4. Strain the mixture into the highball glass, and garnish.

. . . .

Pretty much any member of the orange family will work in this recipe. If you can't find clementines, try tangerines or even grapefruit—and when in season, kumquats, which are amazing in this!

Red Curry & Coconut Caesar

· ·

In Asia, coconut and tomatoes are a classic combination in savoury foods, so I decided to experiment with them, along with some curry paste. This is one of those experiments that turned out really, really well. Never be afraid to try bold new flavour combinations, especially if you get ideas while cooking dinner!

Glass

Rim   Fresh cracked salt and black pepper

What   1 barspoon red curry paste
2 dashes Worcestershire sauce
2 pinches garam masala
4 grinds fresh cracked black pepper
1½ oz (45 mL) coconut water
1 oz (30 mL) rum
3 oz (90 mL) Mott's Clamato Cocktail

Garnish   Red curry chicken on a skewer

How
1. Rim a highball glass with citrus and rimmer.
2. Fill the glass to the top with ice.
3. Add the ingredients in the order listed.
4. Stir well to mix the cocktail, and garnish.

· ·

Green curry paste is always an alternative to the red but will affect the appearance of the drink and the heat level. Be sure to use coconut water and not coconut milk for this recipe.

Garam masala is a unique blend of ground spices that can be found at your local grocery store.

Caesar Picante Caliente

. . . .

Some Caesar drinkers like their clam cocktail spicy—I mean crazy burning hot. So this one is for you the next time you're eating your favourite over-the-top foods that burn your mouth, like suicide wings or spicy beef. *Picante* is Spanish for "spicy," and *caliente* means "hot." No further translation necessary!

Glass

Rim   Celery salt with cayenne pepper

What   1 oz (30 mL) vodka
              4 dashes Worcestershire sauce
              5 to 10 dashes HYH hot sauce (see page 9)
              5 grinds fresh cracked black pepper
              4 oz (120 mL) Mott's Clamato Cocktail

Garnish   Anything that matches the heat of the Caesar

How   1. Rim a highball glass with citrus and rimmer.
              2. Fill the glass to the top with ice.
              3. Add the ingredients in the order listed.
              4. Stir well to mix the cocktail, and garnish.

General Tao Caesar

Using a simple marinade sauce, you can make your Caesar taste like the famous General Tao's chicken. This recipe also works well with flavourings from other classic Asian-style dishes—just substitute the General Tao sauce for teriyaki or Szechwan. Whichever sauce you choose to use, garnish with your favourite meats sauced the same way.

Glass

Rim   Fresh cracked salt and black pepper

What
1 oz (30 mL) vodka
2 dashes Thai chili hot sauce
1 dash Worcestershire sauce
3 grinds fresh cracked salt and black pepper
2 barspoons General Tao sauce
4 oz (120 mL) Mott's Clamato Cocktail

Garnish
General Tao chicken on a skewer
Fresh cracked black pepper

How
1. Rim a highball glass with citrus and rimmer.
2. Fill the glass to the top with ice.
3. Add the ingredients in the order listed.
4. Stir well to mix the cocktail, and garnish.

Smoked Lime & Tequila Caesar

. . . .

The flavours of citrus and smoke are crushed together in this muddled Mexican-style Caesar. The adobo sauce–soaked chipotle gives a fresh, smoky heat that is balanced by the lime and Clamato. The aromatic cilantro garnish adds another dimension as you tilt back your glass to take a sip.

Glass

Rim   Fresh cracked salt and black pepper

What   ½ lime, cut into wedges
½ chipotle pepper in adobo sauce
3 grinds fresh cracked black pepper
1 oz (30 mL) 100% blue agave tequila
4 oz (120 mL) Mott's Clamato Cocktail

Garnish   Lime twist
Sprig fresh cilantro

How   1. In a mixing glass, muddle everything but the tequila and Mott's Clamato Cocktail.
2. Add the tequila and Mott's Clamato Cocktail, and stir well to mix and spread the flavours around.
3. Rim a highball glass and fill to the top with ice.
4. Strain the mixture into the highball glass, and garnish.

. . . .

Make sure you muddle the chipotle pepper well to release its flavour. You can also add a barspoon of the adobo sauce to add another level of flavour and spice, if you like. Experiment with ground smoked herbs and spices for the rimmer.

Valentine's Day Caesar

You can feel the love in this Caesar. The oysters and cinnamon are mandatory, as they are amazing aphrodisiacs. Make this Caesar for the one you love, and let the good times roll! Marvin Gaye or Barry White music is optional.

Glass

Rim Fresh cracked salt and black pepper with ground cinnamon

What 1 oz (30 mL) cinnamon-flavoured whisky
2 dashes cayenne hot sauce
1 dash Worcestershire sauce
4 grinds fresh cracked black pepper
4 oz (120 mL) Mott's Clamato Cocktail

Garnish Fresh oyster on the half shell,
    sprinkled with chopped parsley
Cinnamon stick

How 1. Rim a highball glass with citrus and rimmer.
2. Fill the glass to the top with ice.
3. Add the ingredients in the order listed.
4. Stir well to mix the cocktail, and garnish.

RECIPES

139

Grilled Asparagus Bites with Tarragon Dipping Sauce

. . . .

Serves: 6 Pairing: Mary Had a Little Lamb Caesar (page 41)

C&J: Local asparagus is a true taste of spring in Canada, and this is a great way to enjoy it as a side dish or as a little bite at your cocktail parties. Grilling asparagus brings out its natural sweetness, and we just love the charred flavour that grilling imparts.

Tarragon Dipping Sauce
2 slices white bread
2 egg yolks
1 tsp (5 mL) Dijon mustard
Juice of ½ lemon
1 garlic clove
½ pinch saffron, steeped in
    1 Tbsp (15 mL) warm water
1 cup (250 mL) olive oil
¼ cup (60 mL) tarragon, chopped

Asparagus
2 bunches asparagus
¼ cup (60 mL) olive oil
Juice of 1 lemon
Salt and black pepper

Tarragon Dipping Sauce
1. Remove the crusts from the bread and discard or save for another use. Tear the bread into small pieces and pulse in a food processor until crumbs form. Set aside.
2. In the food processor or with a hand blender, combine the egg yolks, Dijon, lemon juice, garlic, and saffron with its cooled steeping water. Process on high until smooth. With the food processor still on high, slowly drizzle in the olive oil, until the mixture achieves a mayonnaise-like consistency.
3. Transfer the mixture to a bowl and fold in the fresh bread crumbs and tarragon. Season with salt.
4. Transfer the sauce to a disposable piping bag or a large sealable bag and place in the refrigerator.

recipe
continues
overleaf

Asparagus

1. Preheat the grill to high.
2. Wash the asparagus well to remove any grit, then pat dry. Drizzle the olive oil and lemon juice over the asparagus and toss to coat evenly. Sprinkle liberally with salt and pepper.
3. When the grill is hot, arrange the asparagus on the grill and cook for 2 minutes, then roll the stalks over and cook for another 2 minutes. (Alternatively, broil in the oven: spread the asparagus on a baking sheet in a single layer and cook until the stalks are golden brown and the outer edges crisp.)
4. To serve, arrange the asparagus on a platter, with the sauce drizzled over top or served on the side.

Warm Cerignola Olives
with Fennel & Lemon

. . . .

Serves 6: Pairing: Social Caesar (page 123)

C&J: Olives are a wonderful food, but who knew that serving them warm would take them to another level? Try out this recipe—red, green, and black olives, flavoured with citrus skin and herbs—and feel free to play and experiment with the olive varieties and flavourings. This is also a really colourful recipe, so it's nice to have in the fall, when fresh ingredients aren't as available as they are in summer.

2 lb (1 kg) red, green, or black
    Cerignola olives
Zest of 1 orange
1 preserved lemon, thinly sliced

6 sprigs fresh thyme
3 bay leaves
½ cup (125 mL) olive oil
1 Tbsp (15 mL) fennel pollen

1. Combine all the ingredients in a bowl and marinate overnight.
2. In a large skillet, warm the olives in their marinade over low heat. Be careful not to let the oil bubble, as it will overcook the olives. Remove from the heat and drain the olives.
3. Transfer the olives to a platter or bowl and serve immediately, with small spoons or bamboo skewers to retrieve the olives and a small bowl for the pits.

. . . .

The olives don't need to be specific to this recipe. Use your favourite ones. Anything works! Just note that they need to marinate overnight.

Fennel pollen tastes like fennel seed but is much more intense. Look for it at specialty spice stores. If you can't find it, use 1 Tbsp (15 mL) ground fennel seeds instead.

Brussels Sprout Chips with Fresh Lime

. . . .

Serves: 8   Pairing: Smoked Lime & Tequila Caesar (page 135)

C&J: This is the only way to eat Brussels sprouts—especially if you never liked them as a kid. When you fry them, they become very crispy, and frying also brings out their natural sweetness. We then toss them with lime juice, chili flakes, and salt—the lime cuts through the richness, the chili adds spice, and—suddenly—they're like the best potato chips you've ever eaten.

4 cups (1 L) duck fat (from a butcher or specialty shop)
4 cups (1 L) vegetable oil
1 lb (500 g) Brussels sprouts
1 lime
½ tsp (2 mL) chili flakes
Salt

1. In a large pot, heat the duck fat and vegetable oil to 375°F (190°C), leaving at least 8 inches (20 cm) of clearance between the oil and the top of the pot. Wash the Brussels sprouts well and trim the cores. Gently peel the leaves back from the cores to remove them and place them in a large bowl. Pat the leaves dry with paper towel.
2. Fry the leaves in batches in the hot oil until the edges turn golden brown. Drain the leaves well on paper towel, shake off any excess oil, and place them in a large bowl. Toss with a squeeze of fresh lime juice, and the chili flakes and salt. Repeat until all the leaves are fried.

Black Mission Figs Stuffed with Blue Cheese

· ·

Serves: 6 Pairing: Royal Caesar (page 34)

C&J: If you've never been lucky enough to taste a fresh, local, in-season fig, well, you've never truly enjoyed a fig as nature intended! This pairing of the mainly sweet but slightly tart fruit with salty blue cheese is a classic. This recipe also works well with late-harvest pears if figs have yet to make an appearance at your local market.

½ cup (125 mL) blue cheese (Fourme D'Ambert or your favourite blue)
½ cup (125 mL) cream cheese

6 fresh basil leaves
12 fresh medium figs
1 cup (250 mL) sherry vinegar

1. In a bowl, mix together the blue and cream cheeses until smooth and soft.
2. Finely chop the basil and fold into the cheese mixture. Spoon the cheese mixture into a piping bag fitted with a medium-sized plain tip.
3. Carefully wash and dry the figs. Make a small slit in the bottom of each. Gently insert the tip of the piping bag into the bottom of a fig and gently squeeze in a little of the filling—the fig should expand slightly. Repeat with remaining figs. Refrigerate the stuffed figs, covered with plastic wrap, for at least 2 hours.
4. In a small saucepan set over medium heat, reduce the vinegar by three-quarters or until syrupy. Take care not to let it scorch. Cool the reduction to room temperature and set aside in a small bowl.
5. Remove the figs from the refrigerator. Using a paring knife, cut each in half from the top to bottom, dipping the knife in hot water and wiping dry after each slice. Place the figs cut side up on a platter and drizzle with the sherry reduction.

Crispy Fried Gnocchi with Whipped Mascarpone Dip

. . . .

Serves: 8   Pairing: Caesar Sangrita (page 30)

C&J: This simple-to-prepare gnocchi recipe was inspired by a German dumpling that a chef once showed us early on in our careers, back in our days at the Owl's Nest in Calgary. Although these gnocchi can simply be boiled and tossed with butter and Parmesan for a quick meal on the go, we really love them fried, as a snack. Frying gives them a lovely crispy texture on the outside yet keeps them fluffy on the inside.

Mascarpone Dip

1 cup (250 mL) mascarpone
   cheese
2 Tbsp (30 mL) olive oil
1 Tbsp (15 mL) unsalted butter
2 garlic cloves, minced
Juice of ½ lemon
10 fresh basil leaves, finely
   chopped
½ cup (125 mL) grated Parmesan
   cheese
½ cup (125 mL) sour cream

Gnocchi

1 lb (500 g) russet potatoes,
   scrubbed (2 to 4 potatoes,
   depending on size)
2 large eggs
2½ cups (625 mL) all-purpose
   flour
1 cup (250 mL) grated Parmesan
   cheese
½ cup (125 mL) semolina flour
1¼ tsp (6 mL) salt
¼ tsp (1 mL) ground nutmeg
1 Tbsp (15 mL) dried oregano
½ tsp (2 mL) cracked black
   pepper

Mascarpone Dip

1. Using a stand mixer with the paddle attachment, whip the mascarpone until light and fluffy. Set the bowl of mascarpone in the refrigerator to chill.

recipe
continues
overleaf

2. Add the olive oil and butter to a saucepan set over medium heat. Once the oil and butter are hot and bubbling, add the garlic and cook until tender, taking care not to let it brown, as it will taste bitter. Turn off the heat and squeeze in the lemon juice, stirring to mix. Cool the mixture on the countertop to room temperature.

3. Add the garlic mixture to the mascarpone, along with the basil and Parmesan. Using the stand mixer with the paddle attachment, whip the mixture until smooth. Fold in the sour cream, and season with salt to taste. Spoon the dip into a serving bowl, cover, and refrigerate.

Gnocchi

1. Boil the potatoes in their skins. While they are still warm, peel and mash them.

2. Add the eggs, ½ cup (125 mL) all-purpose flour, ½ cup (125 mL) Parmesan, the semolina flour, ¼ tsp (1 mL) salt, and the nutmeg, and mix well until all the ingredients are incorporated and form a dough.

3. Roll the dough into strips and cut into 1-inch (2.5 cm) pieces.

4. Bring a large pot of salted water to a boil and add the gnocchi. When they float to the top, transfer them with a slotted spoon to a baking sheet to cool.

5. Preheat a deep fryer to 375°F (190°C).

6. In a medium bowl, combine the remaining flour and salt with the oregano and pepper. Pour the flour mixture onto a baking sheet. Dredge the gnocchi in batches in the seasoned flour, shaking the baking sheet until the gnocchi are evenly coated. Drop the gnocchi in batches into the fryer and cook until lightly golden brown.

7. Drain the fried gnocchi on a parchment paper–lined baking sheet and season with salt. Keep the cooked gnocchi warm in a 150°F (65°C) oven until they have all been fried. Remove from the oven and sprinkle with the remaining Parmesan.

8. Arrange the gnocchi on a platter around the bowl of dip, with wooden skewers for dipping.

Sea-Salt Pretzel Bites with Beer Cheese Dip

. . . .

Serves: 8 Pairing: Lazy-Long Weekend Caesar (page 73)

C&J: This recipe stems from time spent in Germany during Oktoberfest. The beer and cheese dip—called Obatzda—is made with cream cheese, brie, and spices, and it pairs perfectly with the salty pretzel bites.

1¼ tsp (6 mL) dried active yeast, slightly less than 1 packet
⅔ cup (150 mL) lukewarm water
½ tsp (3 mL) salt
1 tsp (5 mL) golden sugar
¼ cup (60 mL) cake flour
¾ cup + 3 Tbsp (225 mL) bread flour
1½ tsp (7.5 mL) baking soda, for basting
⅓ cup (75 mL) hot water, for basting

1 tsp (5 mL) sea salt
5 Tbsp (75 mL) unsalted butter
¼ medium onion, finely chopped
½ lb (250 g) brie cheese, softened
5 oz (150 g) cream cheese, softened
¼ cup (60 mL) pilsner lager
¼ cup (60 mL) heavy cream
½ tsp (2 mL) caraway seeds
½ tsp (2 mL) paprika
Salt and black pepper

1. Place the yeast, water, ⅓ tsp (1.5 mL) salt, sugar, and both flours in a large bowl and mix for 5 minutes with a hand mixer on medium speed, until a dough is formed.
2. Place the dough in a lightly oiled bowl and cover with a tea towel. Set aside in a warm, draft-free spot and let it rise for 1 hour (the dough should approximately double in size). Divide the dough into 4 balls and let rise again for about 20 minutes.
3. Preheat the oven to 475°F (240°C). Grease a baking sheet.
4. In a small bowl, combine the baking soda and hot water, to make a wash.

recipe continues overleaf

5. Roll each dough ball into a length 1 inch (2.5 cm) thick. Cut the lengths into 1-inch (2.5 cm) pieces and place 2 inches (5 cm) apart on the prepared baking sheet (you should have 30–40 pieces in total). Brush generously with soda wash and sprinkle with sea salt.

6. Bake for 8 minutes or until slightly darker than golden brown. Meanwhile, melt the butter in a medium sauce pot. As soon as you remove the pretzels from the oven, gently brush them with 1 Tbsp (15 mL) melted butter (in total).

7. Stir the remaining melted butter over medium heat until foamy. Add the onion to the pot and cook until translucent but not brown, stirring occasionally.

8. In a bowl, mash the brie with a fork (leaving the rind on). Add the brie and cream cheese to the pot and melt, stirring constantly. Stir in the lager, cream, caraway seeds, and paprika. Season with salt and pepper.

9. Cool the mixture to room temperature before serving, as a dip alongside the pretzel bites.

Summer Melon & Marinated Feta Skewers with Mint

. . . .

Serves: 6   Pairing: Cucumber-Infused Caesar (page 51)

C&J: This fun party favourite combines sweet, refreshing, juicy water-melon perfectly with salty feta cheese. Cherry tomatoes or bell peppers make a great addition or alternative to the cucumbers—in fact, whatever fruits or vegetables are best at the market on the days you go grocery shopping should make an appearance on these skewers. We've paired this dish with the Cucumber-Infused Caesar, since melon and cucumber go so well together.

1 lb (500 g) feta cheese
2 lemons
1 orange
3 sprigs fresh thyme
3 sprigs fresh oregano
2½ cups (625 mL) olive oil
¼ cup (60 mL) white wine
  vinegar

1 bay leaf
Salt and black pepper
1 small seedless watermelon,
  about 1 lb (500 g)
3 Persian cucumbers (or other
  thin-skinned cucumbers)
¼ bunch fresh mint
12 6-inch (15 cm) bamboo
  skewers

1. Cut the feta into ½-inch (1 cm) cubes and place in a non-reactive container. Using a vegetable peeler, peel the rind off 1 lemon and the orange.
2. Layer the citrus rind, thyme, and oregano in among the cheese cubes. Pour 2 cups (500 mL) olive oil over the cheese, making sure the cheese is completely submerged. Cover and refrigerate for 4 hours or overnight.
3. Using a vegetable peeler, remove the rind from the remaining lemon in ribbons.

recipe
continues
overleaf

4. In a small pot, bring the vinegar, lemon rind, and bay leaf to a simmer. Remove from the heat and strain out the rind and bay leaf. Let the vinegar cool, then whisk in the remaining olive oil, and salt and pepper to taste.

5. Using a serrated knife, cut the rind off the watermelon: cut the ends off first, then stand the watermelon up on one end and remove the rest of the rind, starting form the top down to the bottom. Cut the watermelon and cucumbers into ½-inch (1 cm) cubes and place them in separate large bowls. Pick 24 mint leaves and place them in a separate bowl.

6. Onto each bamboo skewer, skewer the ingredients in the following order: watermelon, mint, cucumber, feta, mint, and watermelon, pushing them to near the bottom of the skewer but leaving 1 inch (2.5 cm) handle space.

7. Whisk the dressing to re-emulsify it and pour enough over the skewers to lightly coat. Serve immediately.

. . . .

Both the marinated cheese and the dressing can be stored in the refrigerator for up to 1 week. The skewers can be made up to 6 hours in advance and stored, covered, in the refrigerator. Pour the dressing over top right before serving.

Raw Cauliflower Salad with Feta, Sultanas, & Pumpkin Seeds

. . . .

Serves: 6   Pairing: Apple Shrub Caesar (page 96)

C&J: When people think of salads, they naturally think lettuce and other greens—but in this salad, cauliflower is the star ingredient. The raw cauliflower has sweet undertones that set up so well with the salty feta, and the pumpkin seeds are a classic fall and winter ingredient—toast them to add a lovely nutty flavour and a nice crunch as well.

1 cup (250 mL) white wine vinegar
½ cup (125 mL) plain yogurt
½ cup (125 mL) sour cream
¼ cup (60 mL) chopped fresh herbs (tarragon, basil, oregano, dill, mint, or other herbs of your choice)

1 head cauliflower
8 oz (250 g) feta cheese, crumbled
1 cup (250 mL) sultana raisins
Salt and black pepper
1 cup (250 mL) pumpkin seeds, toasted

1. In a small bowl, combine the vinegar, yogurt, sour cream, and herbs.
2. Wash the cauliflower well and cut into bite-sized florets. Place in a large bowl and add the sultanas and feta.
3. Arrange the salad on a large platter and season with salt and pepper. Sprinkle the pumpkin seeds over top.

Heirloom Tomato "Gazpacho" Salad with Spicy Caesar Vinaigrette

Serves: 8   Pairing: Pineapple Basil Caesar (page 56)

C&J: Everyone loves a chilled soup in the summer, and gazpacho is one of our favourites. We decided to put a fun twist on it by not blending the garden-fresh vegetables into a soup but instead keeping them largely intact as a salad. Almonds are a traditional ingredient in true Spanish-style gazpacho, and they give the salad a nice bit of crunch. This recipe works best with tomatoes but, if you like, use only red bell peppers or watermelon.

½ cup (125 mL) Extra Spicy Mott's Clamato Cocktail
½ cup (125 mL) olive oil
¼ cup (60 mL) sherry vinegar
1 Tbsp (15 mL) Worcestershire sauce
1 garlic clove, minced
Salt and black pepper
½ cup (125 mL) salted, roasted Marcona almonds

2 lb (1 kg) red and yellow cherry tomatoes, halved
1 English cucumber, diced large
½ jalapeño pepper, seeded and finely chopped (or to taste)
1 medium red onion, diced
2 red bell peppers, halved and seeded, diced medium
12 fresh basil leaves

1. In a bowl, whisk together the Mott's Clamato Cocktail, olive oil, vinegar, Worcestershire, and garlic. Season with salt and pepper.
2. In a food processor, pulse the almonds until coarsely chopped.
3. Place all the chopped vegetables in large bowl and toss to mix. Tear the basil leaves and sprinkle them on top.
4. Whisk the dressing to re-emulsify it. Pour just enough dressing over the vegetables to lightly coat them. Toss the vegetables and season with salt and pepper.
5. Sprinkle the chopped almonds over top of the salad and serve.

Don't be afraid to taste the jalapeño pepper as you prepare the salad, so you know its heat level and can adjust the amount as you like.

Crisp Green Salad with Soft-Cooked Egg, Parmesan, & Lemon Vinaigrette

. . . .

Serves: 6 Pairing: Blackberry Lemon Caesar (page 37)

C&J: This is a featured salad on the CHARCUT Roast House menu, where we use escarole, a lovely crisp and slightly bitter green. We've paired it with the soft-cooked egg with the intention of having the egg a little bit runny, so that it creates a sauce when you put your fork into it and break the yolk. We've paired this salad with the Blackberry Lemon Caesar, which beautifully reflects the lemon-vinegar combination in the salad.

1 lemon

¼ cup (60 mL) + 1 Tbsp (15 mL) white wine vinegar

1 bay leaf

1½ cups (325 mL) olive oil

Salt and black pepper

8 slices sourdough bread

4 cups (1 L) crisp salad greens (we use escarole), washed and spun dry

4 large eggs

1 2-inch (5 cm) wedge Parmesan cheese

1. Using a vegetable peeler, remove the rind from the lemon in strips. In a small pot, bring ¼ cup (60 mL) vinegar, the lemon rind, and bay leaf to a simmer. Remove from the heat and strain out the rind and bay leaf. Let the vinegar cool, then whisk in ½ cup (125 mL) olive oil, and salt and pepper to taste.

2. Tear the bread into pieces and pulse in a food processor until the pieces are the size of peas.

3. Heat the remaining olive oil in a large skillet set over medium heat. Once it starts to dance in the pan, add the fresh bread crumbs and cook, stirring frequently, until they turn golden brown. Season with salt and pepper, then transfer to a baking sheet to cool.

recipe
continues
overleaf

4. Tear the salad greens into bite-sized pieces (if small and tender enough, leave whole) and place in a large bowl. Whisk the dressing to re-emulsify it and pour enough over the escarole to lightly coat the greens. Toss the greens and season with salt and pepper.

5. To poach the eggs, fill a medium sauce pot with 4 cups (1 L) warm water and the remaining vinegar and bring to a low simmer. Crack the eggs into 4 small bowls. Stir the water while sliding each egg into the water. Make sure that the water is no higher than a low simmer or it will break the eggs. Cook the eggs for 4 minutes, then carefully transfer them with a slotted spoon to a paper towel–lined plate.

6. Arrange the escarole on a large platter and place the poached eggs on top. Sprinkle the toasted bread crumbs over the salad. Using a vegetable peeler, shave the Parmesan over top and serve.

· ·

The dressing can be stored in the refrigerator for up to 1 week. Drizzle your favourite olive oil over top of the salad tableside for a "chef's finishing touch."

Turkey Breast Porchetta Style with Cucumber Feta Dip

· ·

Serves: 8   Pairing: Thanksgiving Caesar (page 80)

C&J: We love our porchetta—Italian-style pork roast—and we've made a few variations, but this is a favourite for entertaining when plates are not required. This turkey version has all the flavour punches of the traditional dish but is simple to do at home. You can brine the turkey ahead of time, but it should marinate no longer than 24 hours, and it should be kept in the refrigerator.

Turkey Breast
10 cups (2.5 L) water
¼ cup (60 mL) honey
1 lemon, halved
4 bay leaves
1 Tbsp (15 mL) whole black peppercorns
½ cup (125 mL) salt
3 sprigs fresh thyme
1 garlic bulb, smashed to separate cloves
2 boneless, skinless turkey breasts

24 6- or 8-inch (15 or 20 cm) bamboo or metal skewers
1 cup (250 mL) olive oil
1 cup (250 mL) fennel fronds
2 sprigs fresh rosemary
Zest and juice of 1 orange
Zest and juice of 1 lemon
2 garlic cloves
1 Tbsp (15 mL) fennel seeds, toasted
1 Tbsp (15 mL) cracked black pepper

Cucumber Feta Dip
1 cucumber, seeded and grated
Salt and black pepper
1 cup (250 mL) sour cream
1 cup (250 mL) Greek-style plain yogurt

1 cup (250 mL) fennel fronds, finely chopped
1 cup (250 mL) feta cheese, finely crumbled
Juice of 1 lemon
1 garlic clove, grated on a microplane or finely minced

recipe continues overleaf

Turkey Breast

1. In a large pot, combine the water, honey, lemon, bay leaves, peppercorns, salt, thyme, and garlic and bring to a boil. Remove the brine from the heat and cool to room temperature, then refrigerate to cool completely.
2. Slice the turkey breasts in half lengthwise and then slice into ½-inch (1 cm) thick strips. Weave the turkey strips onto the skewers and place in a large, non-reactive container large enough to hold 21 cups (5.25 L) of liquid. Pour the chilled brine over the turkey skewers and refrigerate for 8 hours.
3. Blend the olive oil, fennel fronds, rosemary, orange and lemon zest and juice, garlic, fennel seeds, and pepper in a food processor until smooth.
4. Preheat the grill to medium-high. Remove the skewers from the brine, discarding the brine. Pat the skewers dry with paper towel, then place on a large plate. Pour the fennel mixture over top and toss to coat evenly.
5. Season the grill lightly with an oil-soaked paper towel. Place the skewers in a single layer on the grill. Cook until grill marks appear, then flip the skewers over and continue to grill, until they reach an internal temperature of 165°F (74°C) when tested with a meat thermometer. Transfer the skewers to an oven-safe platter and keep warm in a 150°F (65°C) oven until ready to serve.

Cucumber Feta Dip

1. Place the grated cucumber in a bowl and salt generously, stirring to mix well. Let sit for about 10 minutes. Press the cucumber in a fine sieve to drain any excess liquid and salt. Return to the bowl and add the remaining ingredients, season with salt and pepper, and mix well. Chill in the refrigerator until ready to serve. Crack black pepper over top just before serving. Serve on the side of the turkey skewers.

· ·

Instead of grilling, the skewers can be roasted in a 350°F (180°C) oven until the internal temperature of the turkey is 165°F (74°C) when tested with a meat thermometer.

The Perfect Fried Chicken

. . . .

Serves: 6   Pairing: BBQ Corn Caesar (page 59)

C&J: This recipe has been in Connie's family for generations, but of course we added our own tweaks. It is our go-to summer comfort food, hot or cold. Brining the chicken before frying is a key step in locking in the juices. The savoury spice coating is quite bold, and so we dip the chicken in buttermilk too, which adds a richness and tanginess. But the real secret is frying it in duck fat—this must be done at a very low temperature so that the chicken has time to cook through but still develop a nice crust.

20 cups (5 L) water
½ cup (125 mL) honey
2 lemons, halved
10 bay leaves
3 Tbsp (45 mL) whole black
   peppercorns
1 cup (250 mL) salt, plus extra
   for seasoning
4 to 5 sprigs fresh thyme
2 garlic bulbs, smashed to
   separate cloves
4 boneless, skinless chicken
   breasts, cut into 4 strips each

6 cups (1.5 L) all-purpose flour
¼ cup (60 mL) dried oregano
¼ cup (60 mL) paprika
¼ cup (60 mL) garlic powder
¼ cup (60 mL) onion powder
1 tsp (5 mL) cracked black
   pepper
1 tsp (5 mL) cayenne pepper
6 cups (1.5 L) buttermilk
8 cups (2 L) canola oil
4 cups (1 L) rendered duck
   fat (from a butcher or
   specialty shop)

1. In a large pot, combine the water, honey, lemons, bay leaves, peppercorns, 1 cup (250 mL) salt, thyme, and garlic and bring to a boil. Remove the brine from the heat and cool to room temperature, then refrigerate to cool completely.

2. Place the chicken in a container large enough to hold 10 quarts (12 L) of liquid. Pour the chilled brine over the chicken and refrigerate for 12 hours.

3. Whisk the flour with all the spices and the remaining salt to combine. Divide the flour mixture between two large, shallow dishes. Pour the buttermilk into a third large, shallow dish.

4. Line a large baking sheet with parchment paper.

5. Dip the chicken strips in the flour mixture, then in the buttermilk, and then in the flour mixture again. Shake off any excess flour before placing the chicken on the prepared baking sheet. Repeat with the remaining chicken strips. Refrigerate the chicken for at least 1 hour, to let the breading set.

6. Combine the canola oil and duck fat in a large pot and heat to 300°F (150°C) (this will take about 20 minutes), leaving at least 8 inches (20 cm) of clearance between the oil and the top of the pot.

7. Fry the chicken in the oil in batches until golden brown and the internal temperature is 165°F (74°C) when tested with a meat thermometer. Be sure not to overcrowd the pot. Transfer the chicken to a fresh parchment paper–lined baking sheet. Sprinkle with salt. Keep the batches of cooked chicken warm in a 170°F (75°C) oven until all the chicken is cooked. This fried chicken is delicious served hot or cold.

Tuna Conserva
with Lemons & Thyme

. . . .

Serves: 4   Pairing: Mediterranean Caesar (page 92)

C&J: During our years living in San Francisco, we were introduced to *tuna conserva* at a few of our favourite restaurants. We fell in love with the simplicity of the dish. One day someone said to us, "Isn't that just like canned tuna?" At first we took offence, but after thinking about it for a moment, replied, "Yes, it is, but it's the best canned tuna you will ever have!"

2 cups (500 mL) olive oil
1½ tsp (7 mL) salt, plus extra
    for seasoning
¼ cup (60 mL) minced shallot

4 cloves garlic, minced
4 sprigs fresh thyme
1 lemon, sliced into rounds
1¼ lb (600 g) albacore tuna loins

1. In a tall, narrow pot, heat the olive oil to 160°F (70°C)—you will need a cooking thermometer for this. Add the 1½ tsp (7 mL) salt, shallot, garlic, thyme, and lemon.

2. Season the tuna generously with the additional salt and place in the pot. Make sure the tuna is submerged completely in the oil. Cook for 60 minutes, checking the temperature regularly to ensure that the oil is kept at 160°F (70°C).

3. Remove the pot from the heat and let it sit for 30 minutes. Using a slotted spoon, transfer the tuna to a baking sheet and refrigerate until chilled, about 1 hour. Pour the oil (no need to drain it) into a bowl and refrigerate.

4. Pack the tuna into 4 small Mason jars and place 1 or 2 slices lemon on top of each. Top with the reserved olive oil and seal. Refrigerate for at least 4 hours to set.

5. Serve with lots of grilled, crusty sourdough bread or with a toasted baguette drizzled with olive oil. The tuna also pairs nicely with fresh wild arugula, for a salad.

Halibut Crudo with Citrus & Jalapeño

. . . .

Serves: 8   Pairing: Fireworks Caesar (page 64)

C&J: This dish is super simple to prepare and will be ready in under 30 minutes. Here, we've matched halibut with citrus and jalapeño—halibut is mild on its own, and it lends itself very well to fresh and spicy ingredients—but the recipe will work with any high-quality sushi-grade fish.

Juice of 1 lemon

Juice of 1 orange

Juice of 1 lime

¼ cup (60 mL) + 3 Tbsp (45 mL) olive oil

1 jalapeño pepper, seeded and finely minced

2 slices sourdough bread

Salt and black pepper

1 lb (500 g) fresh sushi-grade boneless, skinless halibut (ask your fishmonger to cut it into 16 even slices as thin as possible)

1 cup (250 mL) wild or baby arugula

1 Tbsp (15 mL) salt, for finishing

1. In a medium bowl, combine the juice from the citrus fruits with ¼ cup (60 mL) olive oil. Add the jalapeño, season with salt and pepper, and whisk well.
2. Chill the platter on which you plan to serve the crudo by placing it in the freezer or refrigerator.
3. Preheat the oven to 375°F (190°C).
4. Cut the sourdough bread into very small cubes and place in a medium bowl. Toss the cubes in the remaining 3 Tbsp (45 mL) olive oil, and season with salt and pepper. Spread on a baking sheet and bake for 5 minutes or until golden brown. Remove from the oven and let cool at room temperature.

5. Remove the chilled platter from the freezer or refrigerator. Shingle the fish slices down the centre of the platter. Whisk the dressing to re-emulsify it, then drizzle half of it over the fish to fully coat. Season with salt.

6. In a medium bowl, toss the arugula with the remaining dressing (or to taste). Season with salt and pepper. Scatter the arugula over top the fish and sprinkle with the croutons. Serve on the platter, with lime wedges on the side.

Italian-Style Pork Jerky with Orange & Black Pepper

Serves: 12   Pairing: Jamaican Jerk Caesar (page 63)

C&J: In Italy we discovered Lonzio—air-cured pork loin—and when we got back to Canada we quickly created a snack recipe to replicate its flavour. The orange, fennel, black pepper, and garlic in this recipe all combine as the pork slowly drys in the oven—almost like a dry-cured pork stick—and the saltiness of the meat screams for a Caesar.

1 Tbsp (15 mL) salt
2 tsp (10 mL) granulated sugar
1 tsp (5 mL) fennel pollen (see sidebar)

½ tsp (2 mL) cracked black pepper
½ tsp (2 mL) garlic powder
1 orange, zested on a microplane
2 lb (1 kg) pork loin

1. In a small bowl, combine all the ingredients except the pork.
2. Slice the pork into ¼-inch (5 mm) thick slices and place in a non-reactive container with a lid. Evenly sprinkle the spice mixture over the pork strips, cover, and refrigerate for 24 hours.
3. Preheat the oven to 145°F (63°C).
4. Set a cooling rack on a baking sheet and arrange the strips in a single layer on top (you may need to use two baking sheets and racks). Bake the pork for 2 hours.
5. Increase the oven temperature to 155°F (68°C) and cook the pork for another hour. Remove from the oven and cool to room temperature before serving.

This pork needs to be refrigerated for 24 hours before baking. Once cooked, the pork jerky can be stored in an airtight container in the refrigerator for up to 1 week.

Fennel pollen tastes like fennel seed but is much more intense. Look for it at specialty spice stores. If you can't find it, use 1 Tbsp (15 mL) ground fennel seeds instead.

Black Kale Soup
with Chorizo & Rosemary

Serves: 6 Pairing: Whisky & Sage Caesar (page 83)

C&J: This rustic one-pot wonder will get you through any fall day. Kale and chorizo and beans and rosemary blend together perfectly, making this an ideal chilly-weather recipe. It's stick-to-your-ribs comfort food that's more like a stew than a soup. A great alternative to the kale is cabbage or shaved fennel, and thick-sliced and charred sourdough bread is a great accompaniment. The Whisky & Sage Caesar combines really well with the spicy chorizo sausage of this dish.

½ cup (125 mL) olive oil, plus
    extra for drizzling
1 onion, diced small
12 garlic cloves, thinly sliced
    (green root removed)
½ lb (250 g) chorizo sausage, cut
    into bite-sized pieces
6 cups (1.5 L) chopped black,
    red, or green kale (well
    washed and dried)
½ cup (125 mL) white wine

8 cups (2 L) chicken stock
2 cups (500 mL) canned diced
    tomatoes with juice
5 fresh basil leaves, chopped
Sprig fresh rosemary
½ cup (125 mL) cannellini beans,
    soaked overnight
Salt and black pepper
1 1-inch (2.5 cm) wedge
    Parmesan cheese

1. Heat ¼ cup (60 mL) olive oil in a large cast-iron pot set over medium heat. Add the onion and cook for 5 minutes, stirring occasionally with a wooden spoon. Add the garlic and cook until the edges are lightly brown and the bottom of the pot starts to feel tacky as you stir.
2. Add the sausage and kale and sauté for about 3 minutes, until the kale wilts. Pour in the wine and cook for another 3 minutes.
3. Add the chicken stock, tomatoes, basil, rosemary, and soaked beans. Cook for about 1 hour, uncovered, over medium-low heat, until the flavours are blended. Season with salt and pepper.
4. To serve, ladle into individual soup bowls and garnish each with grated Parmesan and a drizzle of olive oil.

Place the beans in a large bowl and soak overnight in water before using in this recipe.

Wood Fire–Smoked Steak Strips

· ·

Serves: 8   Pairing: Mustard-Infused Caesar (page 103)

C&J: Butcher cuts are the best cuts of steak: The flat iron is a secret butcher cut from the cow's shoulder blade that is tender and delicious. We added grainy mustard and pickled onions to this recipe because their acidity cuts through the richness of the steak.

4 pickling cucumbers, each 3 to 4 inches (8 to 10 cm) long

1 medium onion

1 cup (250 mL) white vinegar

½ cup (125 mL) water

3 Tbsp (45 mL) grainy mustard

1 Tbsp (15 mL) pickling spice, in a sachet

2 tsp (10 mL) salt

2 tsp (10 mL) granulated sugar

1 cup (250 mL) fruitwood smoker chips (from a BBQ store)

1.3 to 1.75 lb (600 to 800 g) flat iron steak, cleaned (ask your butcher to trim the connective tissue so it is easy to slice)

1 Tbsp (15 mL) olive oil

½ tsp (2 mL) salt

¼ tsp (1 mL) cracked black pepper

1. Slice the pickling cucumbers into ½-inch (1 cm) rounds and place them in glass bowl. Slice the onion into thin strips and combine.
2. In a sauce pot, combine the vinegar, water, mustard, pickling spice, salt, and sugar and bring to a boil. Turn off the heat and let the liquid sit for 10 minutes, then add it to the cucumbers and onion (the liquid should still be hot). Let cool to room temperature, then refrigerate overnight.

recipe continues overleaf

3. Soak the wood chips for at least 1 hour in water, then wrap in aluminum foil, leaving a 3-inch (8 cm) opening at the top.

4. Preheat the grill to medium-high. Place the steak on a large platter and season it with the olive oil, salt, and pepper.

5. Place the packet of chips on the preheated grill until it really starts to smoke. Cook the steak on each side until grill marks appear (about 2–3 minutes each side), then move the packet to the lower rack. Turn the grill to low. Keeping the lid closed, smoke the steak for 10–15 minutes, to cook it medium-rare.

6. Slice the steak into ½-inch (1 cm) thick strips and serve on a platter with the pickled onions.

Stuffed Meatballs with Sunday Gravy

Serves: 8   Pairing: Spicy Pimento Caesar (page 116)

C&J: Chef Joe, a legend from New Jersey, showed us the light when it came to making meatballs and what Sunday gravy really is. You can use different kinds of meats, if you like. Ground dark turkey makes a wonderful lighter alternative.

½ lb (250 g) ground beef chuck

½ lb (250 g) ground veal

½ lb (250 g) ground pork
   shoulder

½ cup (125 mL) bread crumbs

2 large eggs

1½ tsp (7 mL) salt

¼ tsp (1 mL) dried oregano

1 bunch fresh Italian parsley,
   chopped

1 cup (250 mL) ice water

2 cups (500 mL) cheese curds

⅓ cup (75 mL) olive oil

3 garlic cloves, sliced

2 medium onions, diced

2 cans (each 12½ oz/375 mL)
   San Marzano tomatoes,
   drained

1 bunch fresh basil, stems
   removed

Black pepper

1. Preheat the oven to 400°F (200°C). Grease a baking sheet.
2. In a large bowl, combine the beef, veal, pork, bread crumbs, eggs, salt, oregano, and parsley. Slowly drizzle in half of the ice water and mix until the meat becomes tacky and begins to stick to the sides of the bowl. Using a small ice cream scoop, scoop the meat mixture into 24 loosely formed balls and place on the prepared baking sheet. Press 1 or 2 cheese curds into the centre of each meatball. Dip your hands in the remaining ice water and form the meat into round balls, with the meat enclosing the cheese.

recipe
continues
overleaf

3. Bake the meatballs until they start to turn golden brown. Remove from the oven and turn down the temperature to 275°F (140°C).

4. Heat the olive oil in a large pot set over medium heat. Add the garlic and onion and cook them until they are translucent, stirring occasionally. Remove from the heat and add the tomatoes and basil. Using a hand blender, blend the mixture until smooth.

5. Place the browned meatballs in a large roasting pan and pour the tomato gravy over top. Cover the roasting pan tightly with aluminum foil. Bake the meatballs for 3 hours or until cooked and tender, checking occasionally to make sure they're not scorching and that the gravy is simmering lightly. Adjust the oven temperature as needed.

6. Once done, remove the meatballs from the oven and let rest for 10 minutes before serving, with the gravy spooned over top.

Sausage Sliders with Cheese Curds & Tomato Jam

. . . .

Serves: 8   Pairing: Maple BBQ Caesar (page 87)

C&J: When we first opened CHARCUT Roast House, we sold $5 burgers literally out the back door to anyone who responded to our Facebook or Twitter callouts. These sliders are a fun variation on our original Alley Burger.

Tomato Jam
1 Tbsp (15 mL) olive oil
1 medium onion, chopped
2 garlic cloves, minced
1 can (12½ oz/375 mL) San
   Marzano tomatoes
1 cup (250 mL) white wine
   vinegar
½ cup (125 mL) granulated sugar
3 sprigs fresh thyme
1½ tsp (7 mL) salt
1 tsp (5 mL) black pepper
Zest of 1 lemon

Sausage Sliders
1 garlic bulb, papery outer layer
   peeled off, cloves still attached
1 Tbsp (15 mL) olive oil, plus
   extra for drizzling
1 lb (500 g) ground pork shoulder
1 tsp (5 mL) salt
½ tsp (2 mL) granulated sugar
¼ tsp (1 mL) ground coriander
¼ tsp (1 mL) ground white
   pepper
¼ tsp (1 mL) garlic powder
¼ tsp (1 mL) black pepper
Pinch mace
2 tsp (10 mL) water
8 mini slider buns
2 cups (500 mL) cheese curds

Tomato Jam
1. In a large pot set over medium-low heat, combine the olive oil with the onion, garlic, tomatoes, vinegar, sugar, thyme, salt, pepper, and lemon zest. Slowly cook, uncovered, for 3 hours, stirring occasionally. Transfer to a shallow container to cool in the refrigerator. Once cool, puree in a blender until smooth.

recipe
continues
overleaf

Sausage Sliders

1. Preheat the oven to 400°F (200°C).

2. Cut the top third off the garlic bulb to expose the top of the cloves. Place the bulb on a sheet of aluminum foil large enough to wrap around the bulb. Drizzle the olive oil over top the bulb and season with salt and pepper. Wrap the bulb in the foil and bake for 25 minutes or until the garlic cloves are tender. Remove from the oven and carefully open the pouch. Set aside to let cool.

3. Preheat the grill to medium-high. Chill the bowl and paddle attachment of a stand mixer in the refrigerator for 20 minutes. Add the pork to the bowl with the salt, sugar, and spices. Mix on low until the spices are incorporated.

4. Turn the mixer to medium-high speed and slowly pour in the water. Mix for 2 minutes or until the meat becomes tacky and sticks to the sides of the bowl.

5. Line a baking sheet with parchment paper. Divide the mixture into 8 equal-sized balls and form each ball into a patty. Place the patties in a single layer on the parchment paper. Cover with plastic wrap and refrigerate for 1 hour.

6. Cut the slider buns in half and lightly butter both cut sides.

7. Drizzle each patty lightly with olive oil and place on the grill, evenly spaced. Cook for about 4 minutes, then flip over. The patties are cooked when the internal temperature is 155°F (68°C) when tested with a meat thermometer and the juices run clear.

8. Move the patties to a cooler part of the grill and top with the cheese curds.

9. Place the slider buns, cut side down, on the grill for about 30 seconds. Remove, and place the bottoms on a platter. Spread each with about 1 Tbsp (15 mL) tomato jam. Top with a patty and the bun top. Skewer each slider with a bamboo skewer.

. . . .

If you have tomato jam left over, store it in an airtight container in the refrigerator for up to 3 days.

Berry Cheesecake in a Jar

· ·

Serves: 4   Pairing: Mother's Day or **Father's Day Caesar** (page 47)

C&J: This recipe is so simple to make that you don't even need an oven—it is also the best cheesecake we have ever tasted! It is four ingredients, whipped, then layered in a jar with graham crackers and seasonal fruit—and you can use whatever fresh fruit or seasonal preserves you like, to showcase the summer berries and fruits from the market or your own backyard.

¾ cup (175 mL) heavy cream
¼ cup (60 mL) icing sugar
Pulp of ½ vanilla pod
1¼ cups (310 mL) cream cheese
¼ cup (60 mL) graham cracker crumbs
½ cup (125 mL) seasonal fruit, fresh or preserves

1. Using a hand mixer or stand mixer, whip the cream, icing sugar, and vanilla bean pulp until soft peaks form. Scrape the mixture into a bowl and refrigerate until you are ready to fold it into the cream cheese.
2. Using a hand mixer or a stand mixer with the paddle attachment, beat the cream cheese until smooth, scraping down the sides of the bowl often. Slowly fold in the chilled whipped cream until fully incorporated and the mixture is smooth.
3. Transfer the mixture to a piping bag fitted with a large plain tip and layer 4 Mason jars with the cheese filling, followed by the graham cracker crumbs and then the fruit.

· ·

This cheesecake can also be served divided among 12 shot glasses.

French Toast Pie
with Warm Maple Syrup

. . . .

Serves: 8
Pairing: **Pomegranate Caesar** (page 126)
or **My Darling Clementine Caesar** (page 128)

C&J: Who doesn't like French toast? And who doesn't like pie? Our pastry chef came up with this unique dessert and it is the best dessert for when it's cold outside: rich, comforting, sweet, and cinnamony.

French Toast
3 large eggs
⅓ cup (75 mL) 2% milk
1 Tbsp (15 mL) icing sugar
Pinch cinnamon
2 Tbsp (30 mL) unsalted butter, melted
4 slices white bread, cut diagonally

Pie Base
3 large eggs
1 cup (250 mL) maple syrup
¾ cup (175 mL) brown sugar
2 Tbsp (30 mL) butter, melted
½ tsp (2 mL) salt
½ cup (125 mL) all-purpose flour
1 tsp (5 mL) cinnamon
Pinch ground nutmeg
Pinch ground cloves
1½ cups (375 mL) light cream
1 9-inch (23 cm) prebaked pie shell
½ cup (125 mL) butter, cubed
Icing sugar, for sprinkling

1. Preheat the oven to 350°F (180°C).
2. For the French toast, combine the eggs, milk, icing sugar, and cinnamon, and pour into a shallow dish.
3. Melt the butter in a large skillet set over medium heat. Dip one side of each slice of bread into the egg mixture, then fry, egg-dipped side down, until golden brown. Place on a baking sheet, fried side down. Reserve the remaining egg mixture.
4. For the pie base, separate the egg yolks from the egg whites, taking care not to get any yolk in the whites.
5. In a medium bowl, whisk together the egg yolks, ½ cup (125 mL) maple syrup, the brown sugar, butter, and salt. Slowly whisk in the flour, cinnamon, nutmeg, and cloves. Whisk in the cream. The mixture should be quite liquid.
6. Using a hand mixer, whip the egg whites until medium peaks form. Gently fold the whites into the maple syrup mixture until just incorporated. Pour the mixture into the pie shell.
7. Dip the uncoated side of the French toast in the reserved egg mixture and place fried side up on top of the pie. Continue with the remaining slices of toast, arranging them in a fan pattern.
8. Bake the pie for about 40 minutes. To check for doneness, jiggle the pie; if the filling doesn't move, the pie is done.
9. Remove the pie from the oven and coat with the remaining ½ cup (125 mL) maple syrup. Let the syrup absorb before dotting the pie with the cubed butter. Let the pie rest for at least 20 minutes before serving (this is important!). Sprinkle with icing sugar, and serve with vanilla ice cream if desired.

Red Curry & Coconut Caesar

Alcohol in Caesars

Alcohol Glossary

Brandy

The first spirit ever produced, brandy is made through the distillation of wine. Today brandy is produced all over the world in many forms. I strongly suggest you taste the brandy you choose first before mixing it into your Caesar (as they vary in character and intensity), and then use it accordingly. There is no need to overspend on brandy for use in Caesars; inexpensive, good-quality bottles are readily available.

Gin

Gin, like most alcohols, was originally created as a medicine. For the recipes in this book, I use inexpensive London dry gin (unless other-wise specified), for its balanced flavours of juniper, citrus, and spices.

Liqueurs and Bitters

Bitters were first used as an aid for digestion, and they have long been commonly used in food and drink. There are an abundance of bitters that work well with Caesars, available for purchase online. For use in Caesars, look for liqueurs over 30% alcohol by volume (ABV), as they tend to be less sweet.

Rum

This classic sugarcane spirit has its roots in the Caribbean but is now produced around the world. It comes in many different forms: from white, amber, and dark to flavoured rums like the classic spiced variety. Unless otherwise specified, I use white rum for the recipes, because of its sweet, fruity notes, and because it won't break the bank.

Sake

Commonly referred to as rice wine, this classic Japanese alcoholic beverage is actually more closely related to brewing beer. Filtered or unfiltered, and sweet or dry, all types of sake complement the flavours found in Caesars.

Tequila

There are two basic types of tequila: mixto (the cheap stuff) and 100% blue agave (the good stuff). This unique spirit is expensive to produce, but you get what you pay for! So, unlike other alcohols used to make Caesars, this is not one to go cheap on.

Vodka

The most popular spirit in the world, vodka was also the spirit used by Walter Chell to create his original Caesar cocktail in 1969. Because of its distillation process, vodka imparts little to no flavour of its own, so there is no need to overspend on vodka for Caesars. Vodka also makes a great canvas to use in alcohol infusions; see the facing page to learn more.

Whisk(e)y

Irish whiskey is steeped in tradition, and it's known for having a gener-ally light and easy drinking style, which makes it a great fit for Caesars. Scottish whisky (Scotch) ranges from light and fruity blends to bold, peaty, smoky single malts—the Scots produce it all! Each brings a dif-ferent flavour to the party in your glass. Japanese whisky is modelled after Scotch and is quickly becoming recognized for its great quality.

American whiskey follows strict rules, whether it's bourbon, rye, or Tennessee that's being produced, but there are no rules for how to mix it in your next tomato-clam concoction! And although Canada is still better known for our ryes, Canadian whisky blends have become famous worldwide. Whether you are loyal to the Canadian classics or love local craft distilling, Canada produces whisky perfect for Canadian cocktails.

Wine

Wine is made from the fermentation of grapes or other fruits. When it comes to mixing wine in Caesars (really, it works!), you can use it as a base for a lower-alcohol version. Or try using red wine specifically as a float on the top of a Caesar to add an interesting level of dryness to the cocktail, as well as a stunning visual effect. Have fun playing around with different styles of wine, from table and sparkling wine to fortified wines like ports and vermouths.

Other Spirits

Absinthe, Arak, Cachaca, and Mezcal are only a few of the spirits not mentioned in this book but worthy of being experimented with in Caesars.

Alcohol Infusions

Spirits have been with us for hundreds of years. Throughout the ages, people have tried manipulating them by adding different flavours to change the taste of the booze, a process called infusing. This trend has grown significantly in the last ten years, and today's alcohol producers are using almost anything (from classic citrus ingredients to out-there flavours like whipped marshmallow icing) to infuse their alcohols with interesting new tastes.

Infusing spirits is quite inexpensive to do at home, and your homemade infusions will have a more pure and natural taste than most of the store-bought options. Basic infusing starts with a sealable airtight container, preferably glass. Place the spirit and ingredient of your choice (recommended ratios are listed below) in the container, leaving as little air in it as possible. Shake the container well to mix everything together and then . . . wait. Shake the container again every day you are waiting for the flavours to meld, and taste the alcohol to check the flavour progress. After the waiting period is over, strain the liquid to remove any solids. I'll use anything from a tea strainer, cheesecloth, to even a coffee filter to do this. Keep your infusions in your home bar or even dress them up to give as gifts to friends.

Herbs (e.g., basil, rosemary, thyme)

Mix 4 to 5 sprigs of herbs per 3 cups (750 mL) alcohol and infuse for 2 to 3 days (longer will add more colour but bitterness can set in).

Citrus (e.g., lemon, lime, orange, grapefruit)

Mix 1 cup (250 mL) citrus zest per 3 cups (750 mL) alcohol and infuse for 2 to 3 days.

Fat washing (e.g., bacon fat, lamb jus, brown butter)

Mix ½ cup (125 mL) fat per 3 cups (750 mL) alcohol and infuse for 3 to 5 days. This infusion is excellent if you like the taste of meat in your Caesar! Be sure that the infusion is cold before filtering so that the fat is solid and can be removed easily. Filter this infusion through coffee filters for the cleanest-looking infusion.

Soft fruit or vegetables (e.g., apples, peaches, cucumbers, peppers)

Mix 1 cup (250 mL) fruit or vegetable pieces (the fruit peeled and chopped into small pieces) per 3 cups (750 mL) alcohol and infuse for 3 to 7 days.

Dried spices (e.g., cinnamon, anise, coriander seeds)

Mix ½ cup (125 mL) ground dried spices per 3 cups (750 mL) alcohol and infuse for 5 to 14 days, depending on the level of spice you like. Filter this infusion through a coffee filter to remove any grittiness.

Index